Public Administration in Hong Kong

IIII I IIIIIIIIIIIIIII III III III III
I0123744

This book investigates the case of Hong Kong Special Administrative Region (SAR) of People's Republic of China, mapping the changing patterns of political-administrative relations affected by the sovereignty change and structural reforms. It identifies the conditions that account for the varied political-administrative relations resulting from these changes, and develops an analytical framework that integrates and adapts theories and models from Western contexts to explain varied political-administrative relations in Hong Kong policymaking.

The book tests its hypotheses through a qualitative comparative analysis of 18 cases occurring during the period of 1997–2012. It also conducts a comparative case analysis, which identified alternative causal conditions that were missing in the original framework. The book concludes that civil servants no longer dominate policymaking in Hong Kong after the regime change and structural reforms. While senior civil servants have sustained influence over policymaking processes through codified rules and political appointment, some of them have adapted to the changes in political environment that require more proactive policy styles and more hierarchical loyalty to the Central People's Government of China than before.

The first-hand interview materials presented in the book provide insights about internal political-administrative dynamics rarely accessible from the public domain. These insights provide inside knowledge of the actors, structure and processes of local policymaking in a context of post-colonial transition, and will be of interest to public administration scholars.

Wei Li is an Associate Professor at the College of Public Administration, Huazhong University of Science and Technology. She obtained BA in Chinese literature and MPhil in political economics from Fudan University, and PhD in comparative politics and public administration from the University of Hong Kong. Her research interests include politics-administration dichotomy, expert-policy interaction, policy process theories and social innovation.

Routledge Research in Public Administration and Public Policy

For more information about this series, please visit: www.routledge.com/
Routledge-Research-in-Public-Administration-and-Public-Policy/book-series/
RRPAPP

Public Administration in Hong Kong

Dynamics of Reform and Executive-Led Public Policy

Wei Li

Routledge
Taylor & Francis Group

LONDON AND NEW YORK

First published 2023
by Routledge
4 Park Square, Milton Park, Abingdon, Oxon OX14 4RN

and by Routledge
605 Third Avenue, New York, NY 10158

Routledge is an imprint of the Taylor & Francis Group, an informa business

© 2023 Wei Li

British Library Cataloguing-in-Publication Data
A catalogue record for this book is available from the British Library

Library of Congress Cataloging-in-Publication Data
Names: Li, Wei, 1981– author.
Title: Public administration in Hong Kong : dynamics of reform and executive-led public policy / Wei Li.
Description: First edition. | New York : Routledge, 2024. |
Series: Routledge research in public administration and public policy | Includes bibliographical references and index.
Identifiers: LCCN 2023010505 (print) | LCCN 2023010506 (ebook) | ISBN 9781032049182 (hbk) | ISBN 9781032050843 (pbk) | ISBN 9781003195924 (ebk)
Subjects: LCSH: Public administration—China—Hong Kong. | Civil service—China—Hong Kong. | Government corporations—China—Hong Kong. | Hong Kong (China)—Politics and government.
Classification: LCC JQ1539.5.A58 L54 2024 (print) | LCC JQ1539.5.A58 (ebook) | DDC 351.5125—dc23/eng/20230501
LC record available at https://lccn.loc.gov/2023010505
LC ebook record available at https://lccn.loc.gov/2023010506

ISBN: 9781032049182 (hbk)
ISBN: 9781032050843 (pbk)
ISBN: 9781003195924 (ebk)

DOI: 10.4324/9781003195924

Typeset in Times New Roman
by codeMantra

For Tao, Vivienne and Victoria

Contents

Figures

Tables

Acknowledgements

This book is built upon my PhD thesis completed in the Department of Politics and Public Administration, University of Hong Kong. The work is supported by Hong Kong Research Grant Council (General Research Fund No. 740707, John P. Burns, Principal Investigator; Early Career Scheme No. 24613715), Chinese University of Hong Kong (Direct Grant No. 4052231) and Huazhong University of Science and Technology (Start-up Research Fund No. 3004407128). I would like to thank John P. Burns, the Emeritus Professor and Honorary Professor of University of Hong Kong, for his excellent guidance, continuous encouragement and generous sharing of ideas, knowledge and resources with me, so that this book is possible. I am very much privileged to learn from Professor B. Guy Peters, Maurice Falk Professor of American Government at the University of Pittsburgh at various phases of this project. I am grateful for the valuable comments by Professor Lam Wai-Fung (Danny), head of Department of Politics and Public Administration, University of Hong Kong, and by Professor Ian Scott, Emeritus Professor, Murdoch University, to improve this work.

1 Explaining political-administrative relations in policymaking

An analytical framework

1.1 Introduction

Political-administrative relation is among the most important institutions in any political system. The comparative public administration literature offers influential theories and models that describe and explain its variation. In this book, I investigated the case of Hong Kong Special Administrative Region (SAR) of People's Republic of China, mapping the changing patterns of political-administrative relations affected by the sovereignty change and structural reforms, and identifying the conditions that account for the varied political-administrative relations resulting from these changes.

In Hong Kong, the first Chief Executive (CE) of the administration after sovereignty change in 1997, Mr Tung Chee Hwa, was locally elected. He was a business tycoon before joining the government. To assert control over policymaking, he introduced the Principal Official Accountability System (POAS) reform in 2002, replacing civil servant Principal Officials (POs) with political appointed POs (Burns, 2004). In 2008, the second CE Tsang Yam-kuen retitled the POAS to Political Appointment System (PAS), introducing junior rank political appointees under POs. What is the impact of POAS and PAS reforms on the working relations between political executives and civil servants in policymaking?

The case analysis of Hong Kong applies models and theories which were mostly developed and tested in West European and North American contexts, to a sub-national government with a British colonial legacy, a Confucian administrative tradition and a high degree of autonomy in governing local affairs vis-à-vis the Central People's Government of China (Hong Kong Basic Law, 1997; Constitution of the People's Republic of China, 2018; Li, 2022). These theories and models include role-perception model (Aberbach, Putnam and Rockman, 1981), accountability relation model (Romzek and Dubnick, 1987), social structure theory and new institutionalism (Peters, 1987; Savoie, 2003), transaction cost theory (Horn, 1995), political-administrative relations in the policy processes (Kingdon, 1995; Jones, Boushey and Workman, 2006), Expanded Principal-Agent Model (Waterman and Meier, 1998) and Public Service Bargains (PSBs) (Hood and Lodge, 2006).

DOI: 10.4324/9781003195924-1

Chapter 1 developed hypotheses that integrated and adapted these theories and frameworks to the context of Hong Kong. These hypotheses were to explain the reform impact on the patterns of politics-administration dynamics at the macro, meso and micro levels in Hong Kong, and had potential to be applied to similar contexts beyond Hong Kong. The causal conditions and pathways at three levels in these hypotheses were synthesised in an analytical framework (Figure 1.1). The case analysis of Hong Kong shows that this framework is useful to understand administrative reforms in contexts in a non-Western and sub-national government context. This book is based on the ongoing research by the author on Hong Kong's public sector reforms. The dataset includes over 100 face-to-face and confidential interviews, 150 survey responses from political appointees, senior and middle-rank civil servants, non-official members of the Executive Council, elected members of the Legislative Council, members of government advisory and statutory bodies, as well as experts in universities, think tanks and NGOs, collected during 2009–2019 (Appendix I). The triangulated dataset enables the author to gauge the attitude and behaviour of politicians and bureaucrats, and to cross-check the validity of elite interviews.

Chapters 2, 3, 4 and 5 tested the hypotheses through a qualitative comparative analysis of 18 cases occurring during the period of 1997–2012. The individual case analysis was conducted in Chapters 2, 3 and 4 to test and adjust the hypotheses developed in Chapter 1. The analysis found that working relations between political appointees and senior civil servants in policymaking varied from being collaborative, mutually respectful to being adversarial. In some cases, similar career and professional backgrounds smoothed political-administrative relations in policymaking, but deterred policy changes; in other cases, political appointees' agenda encountered inertia and resistance from their civil servant colleagues; in a few cases, civil servants' initiatives were discouraged by risk-averse political appointees.

A Boolean approach was adopted to identify the causal conditions for different political-administrative relations in policymaking. This was followed by a comparative analysis of cases that have similar causal conditions but a different case outcome. Alternative causal conditions were then identified to account for the different case outcome. The synthesised framework proposed in Chapter 1 was adjusted to incorporate the alternative causal conditions and other findings from the analysis (Figure 5.1). The theoretical and practical implications of this framework were discussed.

Chapter 6 concludes that civil servants no longer dominate policymaking after the POAS and PAS reforms. However, Hong Kong's administrative state has been resilient: senior civil servants have sustained influence over policymaking processes through codified rules and political appointment. At the same time, some senior civil servants have also adapted to the changes in political environment that requires more proactive policy style than in colonial times and more hierarchical loyalty.

The findings of the book will be useful for readers interested in the reform of political-administrative relations in policymaking in the core executive. The first-hand interview materials presented in the book provide insights about internal politics-administration dynamics rarely accessible in the public domain. These insights provide inside knowledge of the actors, structure and processes of local policymaking in post-colonial Hong Kong.

1.2 Models and theories

In this section, models and theories will be reviewed to develop hypotheses that incorporate the context of Hong Kong.

1.2.1 Role-perception model

The traditional approach to study political-administrative relations in policymaking is to focus on the formal constitutional roles of politicians and bureaucrats. Political executives have responsibility to formulate policies and prepare laws; legislators possess constitutional power to scrutinise these policies and laws before passing or vetoing them. In practice, politicians, including the political executives and legislators, may not have capability or interest to oversee the details of policies and laws. Elected politicians may care more about winning elections than about pressing for policy and administrative changes in line with their claimed political ideology (Rose, 1976; Savoie, 2003, p. 193).

The role-perception model differs from the constitutional role approach and examines the relations between politicians and bureaucrats based on their perception of each others' roles in policymaking. Pioneered by Aberbach, Putnam and Rockman (1981), the model assumed that an actor's perception would affect his/her behaviour. The model used a grounded comparative method, being developed from surveys of over 500 parliamentary politicians and over 900 senior bureaucrats in Britain, France, Germany, Italy, the Netherlands, Sweden and the United States during 1967–1971. The model has been tested in countries outside North America and Western Europe, including Japan (Muramatsu and Krauss, 1984; Aberbach et al., 1990), Australia and New Zealand (Gregory, 1991).

The role model conceptualises political-administrative relations into four images:

Image I: Policy/Administration. Following Woodrow Wilson's teaching, the image sets a clear boundary between politics and administration (1887, p. 210): politicians make policies; civil servants administer (1981, p. 4). Bureaucrats are of 'Classical' type (Putnam, 1973).

Image II: Facts/Interests. This image asserts that both politicians and civil servants have a say in policymaking, but their roles are different. Civil servants emphasise technical efficacy, while politicians emphasise responsiveness to constituents (Aberbach et al., 1981, p. 6). Empirically, they found some examples in the New Deal era in the United States, the French Fourth Republic and some Latin American settings where technobureaucrats were perceived as guardians of the state against particularistic motives of politicians (Aberbach and Rockman, 1988).

Image III: Energy/Equilibrium. This image proposes that not only politicians but also civil servants are involved in policymaking and politics. However, they differ in styles. Civil servants are tuned to narrow interests, while politicians transmit broader interest; civil servants are pragmatic and risk-averse, while politicians are idealistic and radical; civil servants tend to build consensus and preserve status-quo, while politicians engage in longer-range issues and issues of high-level conflicts (Aberbach et al., 1981, pp. 9–10). In this image, bureaucrats are of 'political' type (Putnam, 1973). Empirical studies show that Image III captures the real political-administrative relations in the process of policy initiation, conflict management, coordination and budgeting in Western democracies, particularly in parliamentary systems (Aberbach et al., 1981). The context of these studies is the expansion of government social and economic programmes and growing importance of interest organisations' roles in specific policy sectors. Bureaucrats' connection with organised interests determined that their policy advice to politicians was mostly small-scale policy adaptations (Aberbach and Rockman, 1988).

Image IV: Pure hybrid. This image suggests that the distinction between politicians and bureaucrats disappears: politicians have expertise, while bureaucrats have political acumen (Aberbach et al., 1981, p. 16). It was said to have a nascent trend of staffing 'hybrid bureaucrats' in the central agencies of Canada, then West Germany and the United States. These bureaucrats' attitudes were different from those in line departments, and their responsibilities overlapped with those of politicians. It was argued that Image IV could mean (1) control behaviour of political leadership; (2) attitudes and responsibilities of civil servants; (3) systematic feature of politico-administrative systems (Aberbach and Rockman, 1988). Studies that applied the role-perception model confirmed that role-perceptions of politicians and bureaucrats had converged although their contribution in policymaking was different (Muramatsu and Krauss, 1984, p. 145; Gregory, 1991, p. 325).

Using the indices developed by previous studies (Aberbach et al., 1981), Gregory surveyed 270 senior public servants in Wellington (Australia) and 210 in Canberra (New Zealand) during 1986–1987, and developed the role-perception model. At the time of the surveys, there were managerial reforms that aimed to enhance efficiency and economy in both places to strengthen accountability of senior civil servants to their ministers. The findings expanded types of 'Classical' and 'Political' Bureaucrats, adding two more types: Traditional Bureaucrats and Technocrats. Traditional Bureaucrats have high level of political tolerance but low level of programme commitment, whereas Technocrats have low level of political tolerance but high level of programme commitment. Different from the original role-perception model, Gregory found that Image II bureaucrats in Australia and New Zealand could be either Classical bureaucrats or Technocrats. Images III and IV 1 bureaucrats in both places were more likely to be Traditional bureaucrats; Images IV 2a and IV 2b were both proactive in developing and managing programmes but the latter were more tolerant of politics.

Image IV captured the politicisation of bureaucracy under the managerial reforms, and was further developed by incorporating managerial theories (Table 1.1). Aberbach and Rockman (1988) proposed that the motives of politicians were to impose direction and control through less unwieldy mechanism than traditional line departments. They also pointed out that the resilience of administrative culture and variability among leaders would prevent persistence of Image IV.

Campbell and Peters (1988) proposed three subcategories of Image IV along the attitudinal differentiation and partisan identification. In Image IV 1, senior civil servants are reactive and defensive in narrow departmental lines or policy field. In Image IV 2s, public servants' attitudes are more positive and proactive. In Image IV 2a, permanent officials labelled as 'career policy professionals' master both policy expertise and bureaucratic cross-cutting gamesmanship. In Image IV 2b, there were two types of amphibians, the 'political careerists' with experience in administration and 'career civil servants' adopting a political role.

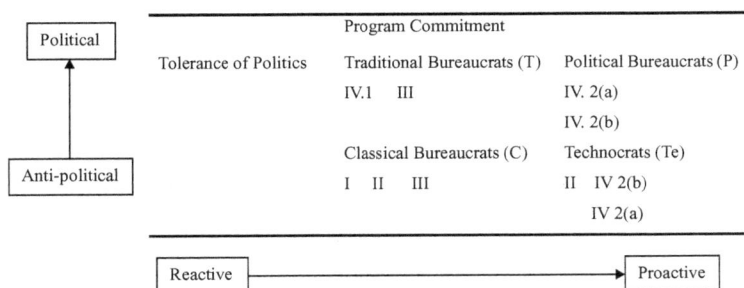

Political		Program Commitment	
	Tolerance of Politics	Traditional Bureaucrats (T)	Political Bureaucrats (P)
		IV.1 III	IV. 2(a)
			IV. 2(b)
		Classical Bureaucrats (C)	Technocrats (Te)
Anti-political		I II III	II IV 2(b)
			IV 2(a)

Reactive	⟶	Proactive

Source: adapted from Gregory (1991) by the author

Figure 1.1 Four images and typology of bureaucrats.

Note: According to Gregory (1991, p. 327), Image II is ambiguous about programmatic commitment. So Image II should be in categories of either Technocrats or Classic Bureaucrats. But the figure in the original paper put Image II in Political Bureaucrat. Here, I correct this.

Table 1.1 Variations within Image IV

	Traditional roles	*Novel roles*
Traditional personnel	Insider politics, bureaucratic officialdom, equilibrium maintenance	Political aspect of bureaucrat's role is promoted
New personnel	Politicise bureaucrats through personnel selection, introduce experts from outside government	Central techno-political role, attract personnel beyond traditional recruitment procedures

Source: Adapted from Aberbach and Rockman (1988) by the author.

Despite the solid empirical basis of the role-perception model, critiques pointed out that it ignored the structural constraints on actors' roles in policymaking (Edinger, 1982; Ranis, 1983); the link between the belief and behaviour was thin (Hodgetts, 1983); little attention was paid to the role dynamics in specific policy context (Legg, 1983), which was acknowledged by the original authors of the model.[1]

1.2.2   *Accountability relation model*

Romzek and Dubnick (1987) proposed four types of accountability along two dimensions: (1) the source of agency control; (2) the degree of agency control.

'Bureaucratic accountability' manages relationship between superior and subordinate within administration, and implies high level of internal agency control; 'legal accountability' manages relationship based on rules and regulations, which is a high level of external agency control; 'professional accountability' manages the relationship based on expertise, which is a low-level internal agency control; 'political accountability' manages the relationship between representatives and the constituents broadly defined, which is a low level of external agency control. Adopting what types of accountability control measures depends on changing institutional conditions (Romzek and Dubnick, 1987, pp. 228–229).

Schedler elaborated different aspects of political accountability such as informing and imposing sanctions, and upholding normative standards. He decomposed bureaucratic accountability into different aspects, such as ensuring administrative expediency and austerity in using public money. He also differentiated several aspects of legal accountability, such as monitoring compliance of legal rules and checking the consistence between the legislative acts and constitutional rules (1999a, p. 22).

Conflicts between politicians and civil servants may arise from their obligations to act according to different types of accountability. Pressure for political accountability comes from the public, while civil servants might restrain themselves (Schedler, 1999b, pp. 338–341). For instance, privatisation of public sector which aimed to reduce public expenditure might risk the financial accountability of managing public resources (Barrett, 2000). Outcome-based performance accountability is not necessarily more effective than bureaucratic and legal accountability (Heinrich, 2002).

Ministerial responsibility was traditionally a central form of exercising political accountability in a parliamentary system. The minister obtained political advice from civil servants without being known. Since the 1950s, there has been tension between ministerial responsibility and political accountability, because the parliament has conducted formal enquiry that named individual civil servants. The practice in Canada is that ministers should not take responsibility for departmental errors beyond his/her prior knowledge (Christoph, 1975; Kernaghan, 1979; Marshall, 1984, p. 66). Verhey (2013) argues that ministerial responsibility requires ministers to (1) give clear guidelines to civil servants what he/she wants to achieve; explain to civil servants what he/she wants and consider civil servants' advice before making a decision; (3) supervise and amend the implementation by providing necessary conditions and take responsibility for the political consequences for the decision.

The separation of policy and politics under the ministerial responsibility is also a myth, because policy analysis is both an intellectual construct and social interaction (Wildavsky, 1979, pp. 114–140). Civil servants were found to be committed to policy programmes rather than be loyal to ministers (Putnam, 1973). British high civil servants provided political advice to ministers, such as how to argue in parliament and how to manage sectoral conflicts. The civil servants have more influence on policy issues on which the ministers lack expertise, time, experience, energy or interest (Christoph, 1975).

1.2.3   Transaction cost theory

The transaction cost theory assumes that political-administrative institutions are the rational choice by legislators to maximise their utilities after weighing trade-off costs and benefits (Horn, 1995). The costs include commitment cost, agency cost, uncertainty cost, decision-making and participation cost in legislation.

- Commitment cost: the cost of ensuring the durable implementation of the enacted legislation after the change of government;
- Agency cost: the cost of aligning the interest of administrative agency to make it comply with the enacted legislation;
- Uncertainty cost: the cost of unexpected compliance requirements placed upon constituents;
- Decision-making/participation costs: the cost of time and efforts required to refine the legislation.

When designing the institutional arrangement, the following aspects will be considered:

- The degree of rule-making authority delegated by the legislature to the administrative agency is positively related to the agency cost and negatively related to decision-making and participation cost.
- The structural arrangement of the administrative agency, including the tenure security, promotion and fringe benefits of the civil service personnel, the degree of autonomy from the legislature and the jurisdiction of the administrative agent, is related to the trade-off between the commitment cost and agency cost.
- The rules of administrative decision-making procedures and resource allocation are related to the trade-off between uncertainty cost and decision-making/participation costs.

Horn added that some exogenous variables could affect the institutional choice, such as stability of the political environment, constitutional arrangement of legislative authority, institutional structure of the legislature, rules of election and party organisation, distribution of costs and benefits among different interests, and the nature of the issues and the legislation (1995, p. 30). In addition, endogenous variables such as legislators' knowledge and cognition of goals and means will also affect the choice of institutions (1995, p. 31).

Horn suggested that the theory could be 'tested' by investigating whether the officials' behaviour was consistent with what the theory predicted (1995, p. 36). In this study, the institutional choice, namely the POAS and PAS reforms, was made by the Central People's Government of China and the CE of Hong Kong SAR government.

1.2.4   Political-administrative relations in the policy processes

Civil servants' relations with politicians vary depending on different models of policy processes. According to the information processing model, the policy process is an ongoing search for goals and means. Career civil servants can influence the search through making trade-offs among competing demands and functional requirements, and through developing administrative structures and processes that attend to particular problems and types of information (Jones, Boushey and Workman, 2006, p. 54).

In Kingdon's multiple stream agenda setting and alternative generation theory, the agenda is set in problem or political streams, while alternative is generated in policy stream. When the policy window is opened either by compelling problems or by happening in the political streams, it's probable that three streams will couple (1995, p. 204). Under this theory, politicians are only one set of actors among others, including interest groups, political parties, public opinions and mass media to have impact on agenda setting. Career civil servants and academics have a great impact on the generation of policy alternatives (1995, pp. 71–72).

Multiple rationality theory rejects the means-end process in policymaking, and suggests that there is no single superior rationality which justifies good policy. Civil servants and politicians may put forward policy alternatives based on different assumptions, values and criteria. They may not share a policy framework and prefer different types of rationality, namely procedural rationality, political rationality, technical rationality and transactional rationality (Kay, 2011).

The nature of policy issues will also affect political-administrative relations in policymaking. Hayes (1992) distinguished familiar and unfamiliar policy issues. For unfamiliar issues, policy communities do not exist and there are no ready-made solutions. These issues are likely ignored or misunderstood until they are forced on the agenda by dramatic performance failures. The development of policy communities for new issues would require new institutions and redistribution of power from existing institution to new ones. Thus, resistance from existing institution would occur. For familiar issues, the development of policy communities over time would provide available knowledge and agenda convergence, and large changes in policy would be possible. Career civil servants may fail to recognise the new problem and resist the development of policy communities for new issues, when they perceive that a problem does not have a ready-made solution from the institutional memory and there is no consensus of knowledge. Even though civil servants may facilitate the changes of existing policy communities, they tend to rely on precedents and make minor changes of policies.

1.2.5   *Expanded Principal-Agent Model*

Traditional principal-agent model assumes that there are conflicts of goals between the principals and agents, and the principal lacks information to exert control over the agent. Other scholars proposed that both principals and agents could have more information than the other party in the initial contracting relation, and share beliefs, goals and risk perceptions (Sappington, 1991). According to Waterman and Meier (1998), the competing principals and agents will have an impact on goal and information sharing between individual principal and agent (Figure 1.2). When there are multiple and competing principals, bureaucrats may ally with some principals who share policy goals with them, but ignore other principals; competing agents may also be motivated to leak information to different principals.

The model implies that for policy issues where attributes of politicians and bureaucrats vary, their relations also vary.

Goal Conflict		Agent's Information Level	
		Little	Much
Principal's information level	Much	Patronage Systems	Advocacy Coalitions
	Little	Bumper Sticker Politics	Principal Agent

Goal Consensus		Agent's Information Level	
		Little	Much
Principal's information level	Much	Plato's Republic	Policy Subsystem
	Little	Theocracy	Bottom Line

Source: Adapted from Waterman and Meier (1998) by the author

Figure 1.2 Expanded Principal-Agent Model.

1.2.6   *Social structure theory and new institutionalism*

Social structure refers to 'the distribution of people among different social positions' (Blau, 1977, p. 27). Structural parameters such as occupation, class position, gender, education, race and social status differentiate individuals' roles, shape their networks and cultural values, and affect the intergroup relations (Blau, 1977). Like social structure theory, new institutionalism emphasises the ideational and structural factors that influence the collective actions, and assumes:

– An institution transcends individuals to involve groups of individuals in a patterned interaction that are predictable based upon specified relationship among actors.
– There must be stability over time.
– The institution, formal or informal, should affect individual behaviour.
– There should be shared values and meaning among the members of the institution (Peters, 1999, p. 18).

Wildavsky applied social structural and institutional analyses to study policy processes. He observed that actors in the policy processes may carry on values and interaction patterns of the institutions (or organisations) they come from, when they are put in an alternative institutional environment; these values and interaction patterns will shape the way they define policy problems and search solutions (1979, p. 395).

Peters conceptualised five models of political-administrative relations based on the social structure and new institutional theories:

– Formal-legal model suggests that the patterns of political-administrative relations are based on constitutional roles. In typical Western presidential and parliamentary systems, elected political executives take the lead in policymaking and civil servants implement policies.

- Village Life (VL) model and Functional Life (FL) model describe collaborative relations between political executives and civil servants on the basis of shared values and goals, and the need to ally against the external interference (Peters, 1987). The values and even goals are not necessarily determined by political executives, but provided by departmental civil servants with strong ethos (Bruce-Gardyne, 1986, pp. 53–73). The models were found in Britain and Canada by the 1960s and 1970s when the economy and employment were strong and inflation low, the government was small, the civil service was respected and trusted by the public, and the media was yet to play a key role in policy processes (Savoie, 2003).
- Adversarial model postulates that political executives and civil servants compete for control over policies. Conflicts arise when political executives want to make policy changes, while civil servants respond by inertia. Other sources of conflicts include differences on policy content (Peters, 1987). Since the early 1970s, when economic growth slowed and inflation rose, bureaucracy had increasingly been seen as a barrier for progressive change when politicians had to face challenges from globalisation and increasingly adversarial media (Savoie 2003, pp. 62–80). Studies based on American experiences show that the causes of conflicts include differences in technical capability, ideologies, culture and time horizon (Maranto, 2005, pp. 38–55).
- The administrative state model proposes that decision-making is dominated by bureaucrats. Political executives and legislature's roles reduce to be symbolic (Peters, 1987). The model explains why New Public Management reforms by outside political executives are resisted by civil servants: when these political executives stress the external and outcome measures in the reform packages, they will have conflict with civil servants' preferences for internal and input measures (Peters and Pierre, 2001).

1.2.7   Public Service Bargains

Another framework to characterise working relationship between politicians and civil servants and its change is PSBs. Under this framework, politicians expect to gain loyalty and competency from bureaucrats, and bureaucrats expect to have tenure, rewards and definite sphere of responsibility (2006, p. 6); civil servants' legitimacy vis-à-vis their political superiors could come from representativeness, high morality, competency, loyalty and blame taking. The degree of civil servants' autonomy varies in different types of bargains (Hood and Lodge, 2006, p. 4).

There are two major types of bargains: trustee-type bargain and agency-type bargain. In trustee-type bargain, public servants are expected to act as independent judges of the public good and possess autonomy. For example, in the consociational representative bargains, civil servants are selected from all segments of society (e.g. through proportionality rules) to obtain representation legitimacy in divided states such as in the history of Lebanon and Cyprus, as well as the federal civil service in the Germany, and enjoy autonomy in exercising discretion that is not subject to elected politicians (Hood and Lodge, 2006, pp. 25, 35, 144).

Trustee-type bargain was most prominent in pre-democracy and colonial settings, and also exists in democratic age because of historical lag, check and balance motivation as well as blame avoidance motivation by politicians (Hood and Lodge, 2006, pp. 29–33).

In agency-type bargain, public servants (agent) are expected to follow the lawful orders of politicians (principal) and politicians, in turn, are responsible for the actions of public servants (Hood and Lodge, 2006, pp. 43–47). For instance, in the Westminster Schafferian bargain, civil servants are expected to loyally serve any government of the day in exchange of autonomy and tenure (Hood, 2001, p. 54).

Hood and Lodge suggest that in practice, mixing of sub-types of trustee-bargain and agency-bargain is possible (2006, pp. 139–140). Recent research in the Netherlands, Denmark, Belgium, Canada and the United Kingdom have shown that with the introduction of New Public Management reforms in these countries, the bargains have changed to be hybrid types, combining old types with elements of a managerial type based on individualism, rather than a full-blown managerial bargain (Steen and Meer, 2011; Visscher et al., 2011).

PSB framework incorporates policy changes that concern civil servants' interests, such as the monetary and non-monetary rewards. When there is regime change, cheating or perceived cheating, the bargain could break down and change. Clear and written rules, shared attitudes and beliefs underpinning those rules, and incentive structure for compliance will help keep cheating in check (Hood and Lodge, 2006, pp. 166–169). Reforms which do not fit the pre-existing bargaining will be harder to implement (Hood, 2002). For instance, when the pre-existing bargain is a trustee-type, with increasing influence on civil servants' career by ministers and civil servants' diminished role in providing policy advice, middle and lower rank civil servants could resist reforms out of distrust in top civil servants to protect the former's interests (Plowden, 1994, pp. 100–110).

1.3   Research questions and hypotheses

The previous studies have suggested experienced strategies for research design: closely relating research questions and research methods (Punch, 1998). I will formulate the research questions according to four periods of time after 1997.

Period I: 1997–2002. This period was characterised as a continuity of governance structure from the colonial era, namely the 'administrative state'.

The first CE of Hong Kong SAR Mr Tung Chee-Hwa (Tung) was the only political appointee in the government administration.

Period IIa: 2002–2005. Tung introduced Principal Official Accountability System (POAS), nominating 14 Principal Officials on contract terms for the Central People's Government to appoint, replacing civil servants to be Chief Secretary for Administration, Financial Secretary and Directors of Bureaus. Many of these POs were appointed from outside the government (see Chapter 2).

Period IIb: 2005–2007. After Tung's resignation, this period was largely a continuity of Tung's administration, because most of his POs remained in the posts.

Period III: 2007–2012. The second CE Mr Donald Tsang Yam-kuen (Tsang) was re-elected for appointment after his first term following Tung's resignation ended.[2] He retitled the POAS to Political Appointment System (PAS) and introduced 34 political appointees, including 15 POs, 10 Under Secretaries and 9 Political Assistants. More career civil servants were appointed as POs during this period than under the Tung administration (see Chapter 4).

The book will address the following research questions:

1 What impact has the POAS reform had on the political-administrative relations in policymaking during Periods I, IIa and IIb?
2 What impact has the PAS reform had on the political-administrative relations in policymaking during Period III?
3 What conditions account for varied political-administrative relations in policymaking during Tung and Tsang administrations?

Based on Peters (1987)'s models, I expect to find three types of political-administrative relations during Tung and Tsang administrations: (1) 'adversarial politics' where politicians and bureaucrats compete for control over policy; (2) 'mutual respect' where politicians and bureaucrats may disagree but respect the roles of the other; (3) 'smooth collaboration' where politicians and bureaucrats share goals and means in policy processes.

Based on Ostrom (2005, p. 59)'s Institutional Analysis and Development Framework, the study proposes to investigate action situations at three levels: constitutional situation (the regime change); collective choice situation (the structural reform); operational situation (actors' background and other issue-based context).

The constitutional situation impacting political-administrative relations is Hong Kong's regime change from a British colony to a Chinese SAR. Before 1997, Hong Kong's political system had limited democratic development. Nevertheless, the notion of 'Hong Kong people ruling Hong Kong' became widely discussed and promised right before and after signing the

Joint Declaration between Britain and China in 1984, and local community's aspiration for democratic participation increased, resulting in increasing demand for political accountability of civil servants in the top policymaking positions. After 1997, the PSB has also changed from a colonial trustee type to an agency type (with sovereignty control by the Chinese government) (Burns, Li and Peters, 2013).

H1a: When the regime change replaces a trustee-type public service bargain with an agency-type bargain, political-administrative relations in policy-making are likely to be adversarial or collaborative depending on civil servants' backgrounds (H3), and issue-based contexts (H4).

H1b: When the regime change replaces a trustee-type public service bargain with an agency-type bargain, a structural reform is likely to take place to emphasise more political accountability than bureaucratic accountability.

The structural reforms (POAS and PAS) have expanded the role differentiation between political appointees and civil servants, and led to varied political-administrative relations in policymaking depending on actors' background and issue-based context.

H2: When the structural reforms expand the role differentiation between political appointees and civil servants, the political-administrative relations in policymaking are likely to be adversarial or collaborative or mutually respectful depending on the actors' backgrounds and other issue-based context.

Apart from the constitutional situation and collective choice situation proposed in H1 and H2, the political-administrative relations also vary at the operational situation. Several contextualised considerations may account for the political-administrative relations at this level.

First, different previous working experiences and educational training of political appointees can shape their values, technical capability and policy styles differently in dealing with policy issues.

H3: Working relations between political appointees and civil servants in policymaking vary because of their different career or professional backgrounds.

H3a: Similar career or professional backgrounds between political appointees and civil servants will lead to their collaborative working relations in policymaking.

H3b: Different career and professional backgrounds between political appointees and civil servants will lead to their adversarial or mutually respectful working relations in policymaking depending on the issue-based context.

The second consideration is public mood, namely the joint attention by public members given to the same unfolding public performance. These public members could be legislators, interest groups or general public who may or may not have close physical proximity. Public performance is often staged in mass media or on the internet (Ringmar 2018). Kingdon's similar term 'national mood' refers to the attitude of attentive public members (1995, pp. 17–18). Intensive public mood, namely high level of public attention, could pressure the political appointees to place and prioritise the issue on the agenda. Civil servants may resist or assist depending on the structural factors mentioned in H3.

The third consideration is the nature of the issue. Based on the transaction cost theory, if the issue is a new problem with no proved solutions, political appointees may spend effort on controlling the policymaking due to high uncertainty costs placed upon their constituents. Similarly, civil servants may resist or assist depending on the structural factors mentioned in H3.

The fourth consideration is the jurisdiction of the issue. Considering the Expanded Principal-Agent Model, when the issue is under the purview of multiple political appointees, the lead political appointee will find it difficult to control subordinate civil servants because the latter may ally with other policy bureaus to object the former. When political appointees choose to drop the issue from their agenda and leave civil servants to manage it, their relations with the civil servants will be mutually respectful. When political appointees choose to press the issue, civil servants may resist or assist or leave the issues to the political appointees depending on the structural factors mentioned in H3.

The fifth consideration is political appointees' capability to handle the issue. Based on the Expanded Principal-Agent Model, when the principal has much information, he/she will have a bigger control over policymaking, and civil servants will be either an agent of his/her cause or reduced to have minimal roles. The relations between political appointees and civil servants will be either collaborative (when civil servants also have capability to handle the issue) or mutually respectful (when civil servants do not have capability).

H4: Working relations between political appointees and civil servants in policymaking vary because of other issue-based context.

H4a: When the issue involves intensive public mood, it will be priority of the political appointees, leading to his/her adversarial or collaborative working relations with the civil servants in policymaking.

H4b: When the issue is new with no proved solutions, the political appointees will spend efforts on controlling the policymaking, leading to his/her adversarial or collaborative working relations with the civil servants.

H4c: When the issue is under the purview of multiple political appointees, the lead political appointee would find it difficult to control subordinate civil servants, leading to the former's adversarial or collaborative or mutually respectful working relations with the latter in policymaking.

H4d: When political appointees have technical capability of handling the issue and would like to control policymaking, their working relations with the civil servants are likely to be collaborative or mutually respectful.

Higher level action situation sets constraints and provides opportunities for lower level action situation; individual actors could affect rules at multiple level action situations (Ostrom, 2005). For instance, the regime change sets constraints on colonial administrative system and enabled the first CE Tung to introduce the POAS reform, which affected rules at collective choice situations. At the same time, the POAS reform was triggered by Tung's tension with civil servants at the operational situations. This shows that feedback from lower level action situations can affect rules at higher level action situations (see the dashed line in Figure 1.3).

I propose conditions at three levels of action situations that explain political-administrative relations in policymaking (see Figure 1.3).

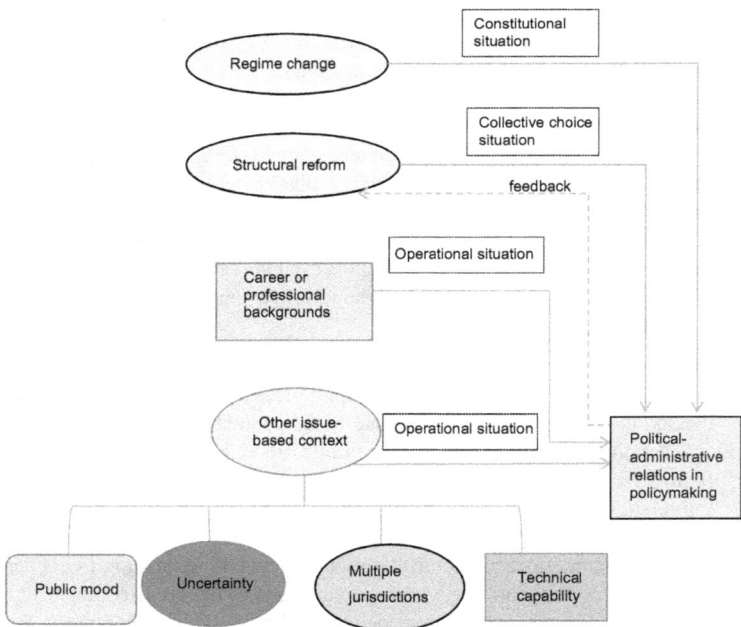

Figure 1.3 An analytical framework explaining political-administrative relations in policymaking at three levels (I).

Source: Author.

1.4 Conclusion

This chapter introduced the research questions, the theories and models in the literature relevant to the research questions, and the context of Hong Kong. It proposed hypotheses and a synthesised framework (Figure 1.3) that incorporates these theories and models, as well as the context of Hong Kong. In the next chapters, I will test these hypotheses by using the qualitative comparative analysis method (Ragin, 2014), and flesh out how varied political-administrative relations in policymaking impact policy processes and outcome. Have the policy processes been more open to community input? Has the policy outcome been responsive to public opinions? I expect that collaborative political-administrative relations will not necessarily lead to more open and responsive policymaking if the involved actors are passive. At the same time, adversarial political-administrative relations will also constrain political appointees from making changes.

Notes

1 They suggested that roles of bureaucrats and politicians in policymaking could be studied through a comparative policy case analysis (Aberbach et al., 1981, p. 30).
2 Tsang was the Chief Secretary for Administration when Tung resigned in 2005, and was appointed to succeed Tung as CE.

References

Aberbach, J. D., Putnam, R. and Rockman, B. (1981) *Bureaucrats and Politicians in Western Democracies*. Cambridge, MA: Harvard University Press.

Aberbach, J. D. and Rockman, B. A. (1988) Image IV Revisited: Executive and Political Roles. *Governance: An International Journal of Policy and Administration*, 1(1), pp. 1–25.

Barrett, Pat, AM. (2000) Balancing Accountability and Efficiency in a More Competitive Public Sector Environment. *Australian Journal of Public Administration*, 59(3), pp. 58–71.

Blau, M. P. (1977) A Macrosociological Theory of Social Structure. *American Journal of Sociology*, 83(1), pp. 26–54.

Bruce-Gardyne, J. (1986) *Ministers and Mandarins: Inside the Whitehall Village* London: Sidgwick & Jackson.

Burns, J. P. (2004) *Government Capacity and the Hong Kong Civil Service*. Hong Kong; New York: Oxford University Press.

Burns, J. P., Li, W. and Peters, B. G. (2013) Changing Governance Structures and the Evolution of Public Service Bargains in Hong Kong. *International Review of Administrative Sciences*, 79(1), pp. 131–148.

Campbell, C. and Peters, B. G. (1988) The Politics/Administration Dichotomy: Death or Merely Change? *Governance: An International Journal of Policy and Administration*, 1(1), pp. 79–99.

Christoph, J. B. (1975) 'High Civil Servants and the Politics of Consensualism in Great Britain.' In: Dogan, M. (ed.) *The Mandarins of Western Europe—The Political Role of Top Civil Servants*. Beverly Hills, CA: Sage Publications.

Constitution of the People's Republic of China (Amended) (2018) http://www.npc.gov.
  cn/englishnpc/constitution2019/201911/1f65146fb6104dd3a2793875d19b5b29.
  shtml.
Edinger, L. J. (1982) Bureaucrats and Politicians in Western Democracies—Aberbach
  J.D., Putnam R.D., Rockman B.A. *Political Science Quarterly*, 97(3), pp. 552–553.
Gregory, R. (1991) The Attitudes of Senior Public Servants in Australia and New
  Zealand: Administrative Reform and Technocratic Consequence? *Governance: An
  International Journal of Policy, Administration and Institution*, 4(3), pp. 295–331.
Hayes, M. T. (1992) *Incrementalism and Public Policy*. New York: Longman.
Heinrich, C. J. (2002) Outcomes-Based Performance Management in the Public Sector:
  Implications for Government Accountability and Effectiveness. *Public Administra-
  tion Re*view, 62(6), pp. 712–725.
Hodgetts, J. E. (1983) Bureaucrats and Politicians in Western Democracies—Aberbach
  J.D., Putnam R.D., Rockman B.A. *Canadian Journal of Political Science*, 16(1), pp.
  183–185.
Hong Kong Basic Law (1997) Basic Law. https://www.basiclaw.gov.hk/en/basiclaw/
  index.html.
Hood, C. (2001) 'Public Service Bargains and Public Service Reform.' In: Peters, B.
  G. and Pierre, J. (eds.) *Politicians, Bureaucrats and Administrative Reform*. New
  York: Routledge.
Hood, C. (2002) Control, Bargains, and Cheating: The Politics of Public-Service
  Reform. *Journal of Public Administration Research and Theory*, 12(3), pp. 309–332.
Hood, C. and Lodge, M. (2006) *The Politics of Public Service Bargains. Reward,
  Competency, Loyalty- and Blame*. Oxford: Oxford University Press.
Horn, M. J. (1995). *The Political Economy of Public Administration*. Cambridge: Cam-
  bridge University Press.
Jones, B. D., Boushey, G. and Workman, S. (2006) 'Behavioral Relationality and the
  Policy Processes: Toward A New Model of Organizational Information Processing.'
  In: Peters, B. G. and Pierre, J. (eds.) *Handbook of Public Policy*. London: Sage, pp.
  49–74.
Kay, A. (2011) Evidence-Based Policymaking: The Elusive Search for Rational Pub-
  lic Administration. *The Australian Journal of Public Administration*, 70(3), pp.
  236–245.
Kernaghan, K. (1979) Power, Parliament and Public Servants in Canada: Ministerial
  Responsibility Reexamined. *Canadian Public Policy*, 5(3), pp. 383–396.
Kingdon, J. W. (1995) *Agendas, Alternatives, and Public Policies*. New York: Harper-
  Collins College Publishers.
Li, W. (2022) Does Politicized Public-Service Appointment Strengthen Political Con-
  trol over Policy Advice? The Case of Hong Kong, China. *Policy Studies*. https://doi.
  org/10.1080/01442872.2022.2133103
Maranto, R. (2005) *Beyond a Government of Strangers: How Career Executives and
  Political Appointees Can turn Conflict to Cooperation*. Lanham, MD: Lexington
  Books.
Marshall, G. (1984) *Constitutional Conventions: The Rules and Forms of Political
  Accountability*. Oxford: Clarendon Press.
Muramatsu, M. and Krauss, E. S. (1984) Bureaucrats and Politicians in Policymak-
  ing: The Case of Japan. *The American Political Science Review*, 78(1), pp. 126–146.
Ostrom, E. (2005) *Understanding Institutional Diversity*. Princeton, NJ: Princeton
  University Press.

Peters, B. G. (1987) 'Politicians and Bureaucrats in the Politics of Policymaking.' In: Lane, J. E. (ed.) *Bureaucracy and Public Choice.* London: Sage Publications, pp. 256–281.

Peters, B.G. (1999) *Institutional Theory in Political Science: The 'New Institutionalism'.* London; New York: Pinter.

Peters, B. G. and Pierre, J. (2001) *Politicians, Bureaucrats and Administrative Reform.* London: Routledge.

Plowden, W. (1994) *Ministers and Mandarins.* London: Institute for Public Policy Research.

Punch, K. F. (1998) *Introduction to Social Research: Quantitative & Qualitative Approaches.* London; Thousand Oaks, CA; New Delhi: Sage Publications.

Putnam, R. D. (1973) The Political Attitudes of Senior Civil Servants in Western Europe: A Preliminary Report. *British Journal of Political Science*, 3(3), pp. 257–290.

Ragin, C. C. (2014) *The Comparative Method: Moving beyond Qualitative and Quantitative Strategies.* Berkeley: University of California Press.

Ranis, M. (1983) Reviewed Work: Bureaucrats and Politicians in Western Democracies. *American Political Science Review*, 77(2), pp. 480–481.

Ringmar, E. (2018) What Are Public Moods? *European Journal of Social Theory*, 21(4), pp. 53–469.

Romzek, B. S. and Dubnick, M. J. (1987) Accountability in the Public Sector: Lessons from the Challenger Tragedy. *Public Administration Review* 47(3), pp. 227–238.

Rose, R. (1976) *The Dynamics of Public Policy: A Comparative Analysis.* London: Sage Publications.

Sappington, D. E. M. (1991) Incentives in Principal-Agent Relationships. *The Journal of Economic Perspectives*, 5(2), pp. 45–66.

Savoie, D. J. (2003) *Breaking the Bargain-Public Servants, Ministers, and Parliament.* Toronto: University of Toronto Press.

Schedler, A. (1999a) 'Conceptualizing Accountability.' In Schedler, A., Diamond, L. and Plattner, M. F. (eds.) *The Self-Restraining State—Power and Accountability in New Democracies.* Boulder, CO; London: Lynne Rienner, pp. 13–28.

Schedler, A. (1999b) 'Restraining the State: Conflicts and Agents of Accountability.' In: Schedler, A., Diamond, L. and Plattner, M. F. (eds.) *The Self-Restraining State-Power and Accountability in New Democracies.* London; Boulder, CO: Lynne Rienner, pp. 333–350.

Steen, T. and Meer, F. V. D. (2011) Public Service Bargains in Dutch Top Civil Service. *Public Policy and Administration*, 26(2), pp. 209–232.

Verhey, L. (2013) 'Civil Servants and Politicians: Problems and Future Prospects.' In Neuhold, C., Sophie, V. and Verhey, L. (eds.) *Civil Servants and Politics: A Delicate Balance.* Basingstoke: Palgrave Macmillian, pp. 25–44.

Visscher, C. D., Hondeghem, A., Montuelle, C. and Dorpe, K. V. (2011) The Changing Public Service Bargain in the federal administration in Belgium. *Public Policy and Administration*, 26(2), pp. 167–188.

Waterman, W. R. and Meier, K. J. (1998) Principal-Agent Models: An Expansion? *Journal of Public Administration Research and Theory*, 8(2), pp. 173–202.

Wildavsky, A. (1979) *Speaking Truth to Power: The Art and Craft of Policy Analysis.* Boston, MA: Little, Brown.

2 Regime change and Principal Official Accountability System

2.1 Political-administrative relations before 1997

Before 1997, the political-administrative relations in Hong Kong government were characterised as an 'administrative state' where civil servants not only held almost all significant local policymaking positions but also perceived themselves as guardians of public interests (Cooper and Lui, 1990). Among the civil servants organised in various general and professional grades, the most powerful elite group were from the generalist grade: administrative officer (AO) grade.

The AO grade (formerly the cadets) came into being in Hong Kong after the Second World War to provide administrative support for the British colonial government's public service programmes such as education, health and medical services, housing and infrastructure facilities. They were competitively selected through examination at a young age, enjoyed high salaries and opportunities to advance to the top of the civil service and even became the colonial governor (Tsang, 2007).

AOs' loyalty to the British government was most valued because they held the most senior positions in the Hong Kong government and got involved in both political and managerial works. Almost all AOs (and their predecessor cadets) had been expatriates recruited from the United Kingdom or other British colonies before the 1970s. Appointment of senior civil servants above Directorate pay scale point 3, including many AOs, needed the approval of the Secretary of the State in London (Miners, 1998, p. 92).

A major political task of AOs was to enhance the legitimacy of a colonial government without Western-style democratic forms, often in response to the pressure of communist forces in mainland China (e.g. 1920s and 1960s). The task involved communicating with the local Chinese population, coopting local non-British economic elites into governor-appointed Legislative and Executive Councils, and consulting these elites on major economic, social and political affairs (King, 1975; Tsang, 2007).

The political orientation of the media and the general public in post-war Hong Kong was divided between the pro-KMT[1] rightist camp and pro-CCP[2] leftist camp (Lee, 1999). The rapid growth of the local population, the 1967 riots and the end of leases of New Territory in 1997 placed great pressure on the colonial government to maintain local stability. When governors such as David Trench (1964–1971) and Murray MacLehose (1971–1982) initiated policies that differed from the old routines of the government (such as establishing local government offices and large-scale public housing programmes, the policies were resisted by civil servants (Miners, 1998, pp. 70–73).

Accelerated democratisation of Hong Kong's colonial government starting in the 1980s was a strategy by the British government to keep Hong Kong's autonomy vis-à-vis mainland China and to have a glorious withdrawal. The fast pace of democratisation, particularly after the 1989 Tian'an Men Incident, such as introducing the direct election of one-third of District Advisory Board members in 1982, enacting the International Covenant on Civil and Political Rights in 1991, introducing directly and indirectly elected Legislative Council (LegCo) functional constituency members (14 and 10, respectively) in 1985, replacing governor with a member of LegCo as the LegCo's president in 1993 and introducing a fully elected LegCo with 20 members being directly elected from geographical constituency (Lo, 1997, pp. 67–100; Legislative Council Commission, 2021), placed pressure on senior civil servants to be accountable to an increasingly critical LegCo and popularly elected politicians (Cheung, 1997).

Some senior civil servants, including the last colonial Chief Secretary Chan Fong On-sang, shared the concerns of the business and industrial community that a democratised and powerful LegCo would harm economic development. Chan even lobbied Chris Pattern, the last colonial governor who introduced a fully elected LegCo, not to allow LegCo to introduce any private members' bill without prior approval of the governor, to maintain the 'executive-led' government. These senior civil servants' stance was consistent with the Basic Law (Article 74) promulgated in 1990 by China's National People's Congress (NPC),[3] and these civil servants were later trusted by the Central People's Government (CPG) to lead the Hong Kong administration after 1997 (Dimbleby, 1997, pp. 366–367).

In summary, during the last two decades of British rule in Hong Kong, the senior civil servants (AOs)' roles in policymaking had been significantly challenged, thanks to the democratisation of district advisory board and legislative council elections, and separation of executive and legislative branches in decision-making and operation. Nevertheless, the conflicts between the last colonial governor and the CPG rendered these administrative elites high stake and significant bargaining power in smoothening the handover. The values and beliefs formed from their colonial civil service careers, such as political neutrality, efficiency, elitism and frugality, have been continuing to shape the policy style of the post-1997 Hong Kong government (Scott, 2010; Burns and Li, 2015). The Principal Official Accountability System (POAS) is a continued effort of decolonising the civil service-led administration and democratising its governance structure.

2.2 Regime change and trustee bargains contested

Tung Chee-wah, a shipping industry businessman supported by the local business tycoon Henry Fok Ying Tung, the media tycoon Louis Cha Leung-yung and the last colonial governor's advisor Sir James David McGregor,[4] was selected by the Selection Committee for Forming the First Government of the HKSAR and appointed by the Chinese Central Government to be the first Chief Executive (CE) (Ming Pao Press Editorial Committee, 1996, pp. 53–72).

Before being selected as CE, Tung was appointed to be the Hong Kong Affairs Advisor by the State Council Hong Kong & Macau Affairs Office and Xinhua News Agency Hong Kong branch in 1992, and a member of the Eighth National People's Political Consultative Conference (NPPCC) in 1993. He was also appointed by Chris Pattern to be the Executive Councilor (EC), probably due to his familiarity with the Chinese government's position (Ming Pao Press Editorial Committee, 1996, p. 113).

Based on the Decision of the NPC in 1990,[5] the NPC Standing Committee established the Preparatory Committee (PC) of the Hong Kong SAR in 1995. Tung was appointed as the deputy director of the PC (Xinhua News Agency, 2018).

The PC formed the Selection Committee for Forming the First Government of the HKSAR which comprised 400 members, all of whom were permanent residents of Hong Kong. These members came from four sectors, namely commerce and finance (25%), professions (25%), labor, grassroots and religious affairs (25%), colonial political actors, NPC representatives from Hong Kong and NPPCC members from Hong Kong. Tung won 320 votes of the Selection Committee, higher than the other two election candidates (Qian, 1997).

The first team of Principal Officials (POs) nominated by Tung comprised the civil servants who used to work for Chris Pattern in the same positions, including Chief Secretary Chan Fang On Sang and Financial Secretary (FS) Tsang Yam-kuen. However, working relations between Chan and Tung were said to lack trust and conflictual even before the start of the Hong Kong SAR government (Dimbleby, 1997, pp. 500–506).

Tung's experiential background differed from those of the senior civil servants, which was reflected in his policy styles and preferences.

Tung's election platform proposed that his administration should not only focus on a stable power transition in 1997 but also long-term sustainable development that aims for building a cohesive society with a strong national identity, a fairly competitive market, and providing high-quality public services for all people. His beliefs about a Hong Kong-style democratic government were also clearly stated:

> The Hong Kong SAR government will carry out a democratic system by following the Basic Law. It will encourage people's political participation, listen to people's views and strive for consensus. The government will not be afraid of political pressure, stick to the long-term goals, shoulder

responsibilities and enhance the transparency of its operation. Although the Hong Kong SAR government will be highly executive-led, it also has many check and balance mechanisms, including monitoring by the Legislative Council, free media, and appeal and complaint channels.

(Tung, 1996)

Tung's beliefs about long-term investment in public services ranging from education, housing and health care to elderly services were not congruent with senior civil servants' value of frugality and short-term cost-efficiency. The pre-handover public service who enjoyed autonomy under the trustee-type Public Service Bargain was now expected to be responsive to Tung's policy agenda (see Chapter 1).

During Tung's first term, Chief Secretary Chan Fong On-sang was said to be a gatekeeper of the whole civil service, and Tung could not meet policy secretaries without Chan being present.[6] Most of these policy secretaries were career AOs and served Patten's administration before the handover (see Table 2.1). Even before 1997, Pattern was said to have banned policy secretaries (civil servants) from speaking to the ECs appointed by Tung.[7] These

Table 2.1 Principal officials (policy secretaries) of HKSARG in July 1997

Name	Career background	Position titles immediately before and after July 1997
Chan Fong On-sang	Joined government Administrative Service (AO) in 1962	Chief Secretary for Administration, November 1993–April 2000
Tsang Yam-kuen	Joined government Administrative Service in 1971	Financial Secretary, September 1995–April 2001
Leung Oi-sie	Law firm partner and solicitor	Secretary for Justice, July 1997–October 2005
Suen Ming-yeung	Joined government Administrative Service in 1966	Temporary secondment to the Chief Executive's Office as the Secretary for Policy Co-ordination; resumed the post as Secretary for Home Affairs in July 1997; Secretary for Constitutional Affairs, August 1997–June 2002
Chau Tak-hay	Retired from government as AO Staff A1	Secretary for Broadcasting, Culture and Sport, November 1995–March 1998
Siu Kwing-chue	Joined government Administrative Service in 1966	Secretary for Transport, 1996–July 1997; Head of Central Policy Unit, August 1997–November 1998; Secretary for Planning, Environment and Lands, November 1998–July 2001.

(continued)

Table 2.1 (Continued)

Name	Career background	Position titles immediately before and after July 1997
Nicholas Ng Wing-fui	Joined government Administrative Service in 1971	Secretary for Constitutional Affairs, January 1994–August 1997 Secretary for Transport , August 1997–April 2002
Dominic Wong Shing-wah	Joined government Administrative Service in 1973	Secretary for Housing, December 1994–April 2002
Fok Lo Shiu-ching	Joined government Administrative Service in 1962	Secretary for Health and Welfare, September 1994–September 1999
Hui Si-yan	Joined government Administrative Service in 1971	Secretary for Financial Services, 1995–June 2000
Wong Wing-ping	Joined government Administrative Service in 1973	Secretary for Education and Manpower, 1995–July 2000
Lai Hing-ling	Joined government Administrative Service in 1973	Secretary for Security, February 1995–August 1998
Leung Po-wing	Joined government Administrative Service in June 1973	Secretary for Planning, Environment and Lands, May 1995–November 1998
Kwong Ki-chi	Joined government Administrative Service in 1978	Secretary for the Treasury, April 1995–April 1998
Yue Chung-yee	Joined government Administrative Service in 1974	Secretary for Trade and Industry, 1995–1998
Lam Woon-kwong	Joined government Administrative Service in 1974	Secretary for the Civil Service, February 1996–June 2000
Ip Shu-kwan	Joined government Administrative Service in 1973	Secretary for Economic Services, June 1996–May 2000
Kwong Hon-sang	Joined government as an Apprentice Engineer in 1963	Secretary for Works, October 1995–July 1999

Source: Government press releases; biography webpages and government archives (http://www.ceo.gov.hk/eng/biography.htm; https://www.basiclaw.gov.hk/filemanager/content/en/files/anniversary-reunification15/anniversary-reunification15-ch1-5.pdf).

ECs include two non-career civil servant professionals, Elsie Leung Oi Sie and Antony Leung Kam-chung, who were later appointed as the Secretary for Justice and FS, respectively, for the first SAR government. Lacking smooth communication and collaboration between Tung and the senior civil service resulted in inadequate support by the latter to carry out Tung's policy plans.

As one former permanent secretary (PS) in Tung's administration articulated how regime change brought about clashes between 'outsiders' and 'insiders':

> But they [Tung's first Executive Council][8] were still doing in dues, a lot of great ideas of what was going to happen. We gonna make them up. ...The bureaucracy responded to relatively bright ideas saying: yes, bright ideas, but changes, first of all, it takes time, second of all, have you thought about the constituency you are dealing with? ...In reality, as was portrayed in the press, there was a clash between the new ExCo [Executive Council] and senior officials of pre-transition arrangement.[9]

According to this civil servant, the clashes were not merely caused by miscommunication but were related to the political team's top-down policy-making style that reduced senior civil servants' role in formulating policies:

> In the pure bureaucratic pre-97, the tradition was once someone had some bright ideas, normally it will go to the middle level of management to see how one would execute that policy. It is necessary to take down to the frontline, say supposing we did this, how would it happen? You would test it for execution. You would consult it and get the conclusion. You would test it before you tried to do it. This is the old way. The new way, as it began, was to come up an idea and forget all about it. Excuse me, sir.[10]

Another source of political-administrative friction originates from different orientation of generalist AOs who are posted to different departments and branches of the Government Secretariat throughout their career, and professional grade officers who often spend their career in one department (Miners, 1998, p. 91).

2.2.1 Case 2.1: Increasing housing supply

One instance to illustrate adversarial political-administrative relations during 1997–2002 is the housing policy. Hong Kong's private domestic property rental indices rose from 92.4 to 127.4 during January 1993–January 1997.[11] High property prices not only affected the living quality of residents but also the international competitiveness of Hong Kong's businesses (Hong Kong Consumer Council, 1996). On the goal of increasing homeownership to 70% and building at least 85,000 housing flats annually over ten years announced by Tung on 1 July 1997,[12] Dominic Wong Shing-wah, the then Secretary for Housing, appeared not to be aware of the goal until he heard it from Tung's announcement.[13]

From the perspective of civil servants, however, politically it is not wise to publicly commit to a specific policy target before making sure that the target is deliverable. The then Chief Secretary tried to persuade Tung to reduce the target from 100,000 to 85,000.[14] In the case of dramatically increasing housing supply, not only was it an administrative challenge to realise the target, but also politically it turned out to be more and more unfeasible due to the sharp decline of housing prices associated with the unexpected Asian Financial Crisis. The corruption found in private contractors building public housing estates, and over 100,000 home buyers with huge financial debts in the peak of economic recession greatly eroded public confidence in the policy (Lau, 2002). In 1999, the Land Sale Programme led by the government was supplemented by a market-led Application List System and even government land sales were suspended when the economic recession went deep during the 2003 SARs epidemic, effectively reducing the housing supply.[15]

Based on Case 2.1, H1a, H3b and H4a are confirmed; the following hypothesis is put forward:

> Under the structural role differentiation between political appointees(the CE in this case) and civil servants (the secretary in this case), the political-administrative relations in policy-making are likely to be adversarial: 1) when political appointees and civil servants have different career backgrounds; and 2) the issue involves intensive public mood.

2.2.2   *Case 2.2: Education reform*

In the case of education reform, the adversarial political-administrative relations reflect more of the conflicts between political appointees and professional grade officers. In 2000, Tung put forward a comprehensive education reform plan covering all stages of lifetime education, to prepare future generations for a knowledge-based economy and a more developed China.[16] The reforms aimed at strengthening quality control over schools' education by introducing performance indicators and respecting learning diversity (Chan, 2000). Apart from devoting more resources to these sectors, there were initiatives to change the curriculum and teaching methods, such as changing the medium of instruction from English to Chinese to teach all non-English subjects starting from 1998. But these reforms were not welcomed by school teachers who believed a more flexible use of a medium of instruction for different subjects be adopted. With a hasty timetable to implement the new initiative across the board,[17] not sufficient quality Chinese textbooks for various subjects were available to assist teaching, which was frustrating and affected teachers. Teachers and parents were also worried about students' declining English language proficiency after the policy change.[18] In the Education Department, education officers were said to be sympathetic with some critical school professionals and not proactive in formulating implementation plans for the reform. Merging the education department with the education bureau in 2002 was in part to smooth the reform implementation.[19]

Based on Case 2.2, H2, H3b, H4a, H4b and H4d are confirmed; the following hypothesis is proposed:

> Under the structural role differentiation between political appointees and civil servants (the CE in this case), the political-administrative relations in policymaking are likely to be adversarial 1) when political appointees and civil servants have similar professional backgrounds; 2) when political appointees have technical capability of handling the issue; 3) when the issue is new with no proved solutions; and 4) the public mood is intensive.

2.3 Political and economic contexts before the POAS reform (1997–2002)

Apart from the roles of civil servants, several environmental factors explain why Tung's policy initiatives were difficult to implement.

2.3.1 Declining popularity and conflictual relations with the pro-democracy camp

Politically, public satisfaction with government performance declined during 1997–2002, particularly in aspects of maintaining economic prosperity (from 44.3% to 14.2%) and improving people's livelihood (29%–17%). Tung's conflictual relations with pro-democracy political parties,[20] which still managed to obtain 62.3% popular votes and 18 out of 60 seats in the first LegCo election after 1997,[21] were not helpful to obtain public support for his policy initiatives. Tung's reversal of local electoral reforms adopted by Chris Pattern, and the change of electoral rules for the Legislative Council elections, restricted party politics (Cheung, 2002) and fell short of the demand for direct election of more LegCo members and the CE by the pro-democracy camp.[22] With the continued distrust by some public members and the pro-democracy camp towards the CPG, Tung's policy initiatives were often perceived as interventions by the latter and resisted by the local community.

For instance, the use of Chinese as a medium of instruction in secondary schools was introduced by the government as early as 1984 and was supported by educational research evidence as being effective to improve students' learning (Yan, 2001). However, its implementation in 1998 was perceived by some as a decolonisation tool (Tsang, 2006). As a senior civil servant involved in the policy decision affirmed:

> The policy was, on the one hand, to persuade them to switch to mother tongue teaching for those who can't teach in English. But at the same time, the government would give additional resources to try to improve the standard of English of the teachers so that eventually they can move back to English teaching. That was the way the policy was drafted. The

policy was not like it was made out by some people that suddenly after 1997 became politically incorrect to teach in English.[23]

2.3.2   Case 2.3: Decision not to prosecute Aw Sian

Similarly, the controversies concerning the Department of Justice's decision not to prosecute Sally Aw Sian, a member of the Chinese Political Consultative Conference, were related to the distrust of CPG and contestation over the legal system by the pro-democracy camp. Aw Sian, the owner of several newspapers, was suspected to have co-conspired with her subordinate to inflate newspaper circulations and defraud advertisers. The then Secretary for Justice Leung Oi-sie, a former lawyer in private practice, was under political pressure to explain the bases of the decision not to prosecute Aw Sian to the public, even when the other defendants were still on trial.[24] After the trial was completed, Leung made a statement in the LegCo panel that explained the bases of her decision, namely (1) insufficient evidence; (2) public interest in respect of preventing unemployment in times of economic recession. Such an action was unprecedented, given the well-established policy that the reasons for prosecution decisions were not disclosed.[25]

However, Leung's reasoning, particularly the public interest consideration, was not accepted by pro-democracy camp legislators, bar associations and some legal academics, who believed that the Chinese government played a role in the decision.[26] A motion of no-confidence was moved by a Democratic Party (DP) legislator elected from the legal functional constituency. As Leung's immediate subordinate Director of Public Prosecutions (DPP) admitted, although the public interest consideration was already established in the prosecution policy before 1997, the factor of unemployment never occurred to him as a factor of public interest consideration before. DPP then consulted overseas prosecutors, most of whom were convinced that unemployment could be a factor of public interest consideration in prosecution decisions (Cliff, 2009).

In this case, the outsider Secretary for Justice and the DPP had different career backgrounds but both received legal training. Their similar professional backgrounds helped smooth their working relations to tide over the hostile political environment. Even though DPP had a different professional opinion in the earlier stage of decision-making, he respected and supported Secretary's alternative judgement. Their working relations can be characterised as being 'mutually respectful'.

Based on Case 2.3, H1a, H3b and the Functional Life Model,[27] the following hypothesis is proposed:

> When the regime change replaces a trustee-type public service bargain with an agency-type bargain, political-administrative relations are likely to be mutually respectful (1) when politicians have different career background but similar professional background with civil servants; (2) when the public mood is antagonistic towards the government.

2.3.3 Economic recession and civil service reforms

Economically, the Asian Financial Crisis that hit Thailand hard also spread to Hong Kong's stock market and currency. Although Hong Kong Dollar remained strong, thanks to Monetary Authority's intervention, the Hang Seng index declined 60% or so from August 1997–August 1998 (Jao, 2001). The GDP growth rate was −5.1% in real terms, the unemployment rate rose from 2.2% to 5.8% during July 1997–1998. [28] The price index of the domestic property market declined from 172.9 in October 1997 to 95.6 in October 1998.[29]

The government adopted measures to cushion the economic impact on public finance, such as freezing civil service pay adjustment and open recruitment in 1999–2000,[30] downsizing 9,774 civil service posts through the first voluntary retirement scheme during July 2000–June 2002,[31] and retiring ten directorate civil servants under the Management-Initiated Retirement Scheme during September 2000–February 2002.[32] The government also privatised facilities of public housing estates and water supplies. The civil service reforms were protested and court actions were taken by various civil service unions over pay cuts, privatisation plans and localisation (Burns, 2004, pp. 306–307).

2.4 POAS reform and change of government policy processes

The introduction of POAS is a response to the demand of the pro-democracy camp to introduce a 'ministerial system'[33] and to address the public dissatisfaction towards ineffective public services (Scott, 2010, pp. 51–53). It is a top-down programme of politicisation and bureaucratisation initiated by Tung Chee-hwa to respond to the public demands for a more economic, accountable and responsive civil service together with the demands for a more effective and accountable political executive (Painter, 2005). The reform changed the employment term of Chief Secretary for Administration (CSA), FS and directors of bureaus (former policy secretaries) from civil servants to political appointees (POs). The most senior civil servants in policy bureaus, still retaining the rank of Directorate Grade 8 as before the reform, were titled PSs, and were under the Directors of bureaus in the hierarchy.

In Tung's re-election speech, he explained the rationale for introducing the POAS, namely to emphasise political accountability and make civil service in tune with societal changes:

> Through a more accountable system, the senior officials will become more answerable in their service to the community. In addition, we believe that it will foster an accountability culture within the entire civil service that is more in tune with the times.
>
> (Beijing Time, 2001)

The reform enabled the CE Tung to select personnel who supported his vision and agenda. Under the POAS, Tung reappointed two outsiders, namely Secretary for Justice Leung Oi-sie and Secretary for Health and Welfare (SHW) Dr Eng Kiong Yeoh, the former CE of the Hospital Authority. CE also appointed five new personnel from outside civil service, including two bankers as FS and Secretary for Financial Services and Treasury (SFST), a medical professor and university vice-chancellor as the Secretary for Education and Manpower, an environmental engineer as the Secretary for Environment, Transport and Works, and an ophthalmologist as Secretary for Home Affairs (SHA).

The PO team was made of financial and professional elites who supported Tung's proactive policy reform agenda ranging from education to housing, and shared his commitment to the nation. First, FS Leung Kam-chung assisted in the first election campaign of Tung and served as a member of ExCo in the first Tung administration before joining the PO team. He also chaired the Education Commission, which was entrusted by Tung to review the education system and proposed to change the 'exam-oriented' system to a system that emphasises life-long and all-around learning, and 'commitment to the families, society, nation, and the world at large'.[34] SFST Ma Si-hang was a close friend of Leung and was invited by Tung to join the PO team through Leung's introduction. Some of them also embraced cost-efficient and outcome-based approaches to manage public service delivery (see Chapter 3). SHA Patrick Ho Chi Ping was said to be eager to make an integrated cultural policy that could bring Hong Kong people closer to China.[35]

The reform changed government policy processes, enabling the CE to directly access directors of bureaus (former policy secretaries) without going through the CSA. The policy coordination role was taken away from the CSA and policy committee to the CE's office under the POAS. The Director of CE's office, a politically appointed PO was introduced to '*liaise and coordinate policy issues with members of the political team*'.[36]

The POs under the POAS were appointed to the ExCo chaired by the CE, to '*participate directly in policymaking at the highest level*', and to '*take part in setting priorities for policy and legislative initiatives, and in deciding on the allocation of resources for the government as a whole*'.[37] In other words, the role of the ExCo was more like the Cabinet under the Westminster-style ministerial system, compared to the colonial government and the first Tung administration when the head of policy bureaus needed to get approval from the CSA before placing a paper on ExCo's agenda.[38]

As one former senior civil servant commented:

The whole purpose of having this policy committee [before the POAS] was for issues to be threshed out for all interested policy secretaries, for everybody had an opportunity to explain their position, and defend, and then for a consensus to be reached.... Some policies were thrown back because they were half-baked. Sometimes CS[A] overruled the policy sec-retaries.... [Under the POAS], all policy secretaries plus three super secre-taries, all work to him[CE], ...the policy committee no longer worked. ... policy secretaries soon learn how to lobby CE directly.[39]

Another former senior civil servant and PO confirmed:

In the first term of Tung's office, they followed the old system, meaning that the Chief Secretary is the real no.2 in the government. But after the 2002 transition, that become blurred. Nobody is sure what the exact role of CS[A] and FS. Now FS still has a very clear-cut area, like the budget, and the economic side of it. That's fairly well easily defined. The CS[A] easily overlaps the CE. ...But then when the CSA's role became blurred, the CE office's director's role became even more blurred.[40]

The CSA Chan Fong On-sang protested the introduction of the POAS, and resigned in 2001. In her last major speech, she expressed her belief that a clean and politically neutral civil service recruited based on intellectual abil-ity rather than political patronage, was critical to Hong Kong's stability and prosperity. Therefore, '*they must endure and survive every fad or fashion or paradigm shift that comes our way*'.[41]

In conclusion, the POAS reform introduced both new roles (politically appointed POs) and new personnel (bankers and professionals from outside the government). As Image IV suggests (see Chapter 1), the outsider politi-cal appointees are expected to play a central techno-political role after the POAS reform. Based on the Expanded Principal-Agent Model and cases of political-administrative relations in the first Tung administration, the study expects varied political-administrative relations due to a different level of information possessed by POs and senior civil servants dealing with various policy issues.

After tracing the processes of regime change and introduction of the POAS, H1b can be confirmed, namely:

When the regime change replaces a trustee-type public service bargain with an agency-type bargain, structural reform is likely to take place to emphasise more political accountability than bureaucratic accountability.

H1b can be further adjusted to include the change of government policy pro-cesses in the context of decolonisation, namely H1c:

When the regime change from colonial government replaces a trustee-type public service bargain with an agency-type bargain, structural reform is likely to take place to shift policymaking roles from civil servants to politi-cal executives.

Notes

1 KMT refers to Kuo Min Tang, the ruling political party of mainland China during 1927–1949 and was founded by Sun Yat-sen in 1912, to end the rule by Qing dynasty. KMT under Chiang Kai-shek was in war with the Communist Party of China during 1945–1949, and moved to Taiwan after losing the war. https://www.britannica.com/topic/Nationalist-Party-Chinese-political-party Access on 11 August 2021.

2 Chinese Communist Party.

3 Basic Law of the Hong Kong Special Administrative Region of the People's Republic of China. https://www.basiclaw.gov.hk/en/basiclaw/chapter1.html

4 He used to be government official, the director of the Hong Kong General Chamber of Commerce, and elected member of LegCo. He supported the LegCo electoral reform bill by the last governor Christopher Francis Patten and was appointed as his Executive Councilor.

5 Decision of the National People's Congress on the Method for the Formation of the First Government and the First Legislative Council of the Hong Kong Special Administrative Region. The Decision was adopted at the Third Session of the Seventh National People's Congress on 4 April 1990. https://www.elegislation.gov.hk/hk/capA202

6 Interview with a former senior civil servant, 8 January 2010.

7 Interview with a former senior civil servant, 4 August 2009.

8 The phrase in the bracket is added by the author. This applies to all brackets in the quotes of this book.

9 Interview with a former senior civil servant, 4 August 2009.

10 See note 9.

11 Private Domestic - Rental Indices by Class (Territory-wide) (from 1979). Hong Kong Government Rating and Valuation Department. https://www.rvd.gov.hk/en/property_market_statistics/index.html

12 1997 Policy Programme, Housing Bureau.

13 Interview with a former civil servant, 8 January 2010.

14 Interview with a former senior civil servant, 18 October 2010.

15 Legislative Council Secretariat. Information Note: Land Supply in Hong Kong https://www.legco.gov.hk/yr05-06/english/sec/library/0506in20e.pdf

16 Tung Chi Hwa, 2000 Policy Address. https://www.info.gov.hk/gia/general/200010/11/1011140.htm

17 Starting from 1998/1999 school year, only 112 out of 400 or so public funded schools were permitted to teach non-language subjects in English. Legislative Council Secretariat Information Note EMB(EC) 101/55/1/C. https://www.legco.gov.hk/yr04-05/chinese/panels/ed/papers/emb_ec_101_55_1_c_c.pdf.

18 Centre for Advancement of Chinese Language Education and Research, The University of Hong Kong. The status and prospect of medium of instruction-Voices of three thousand educating staff 教学语言的现况与前瞻——三千教育工作者的心声. http://www.cacler.hku.hk/site/assets/files/2073/04_moirpt_nov2005_cht.pdf.

19 Interview with a former senior civil servant, 30 July 2009.

20 'Pro-democracy political parties' include Democratic Party, the Frontier and Citizens Party. Other political parties elected to the LegCo include Democratic Alliance for the Betterment and Progress of Hong Kong(DAB), Liberal Party (LP) and Hong Kong Progressive Alliance (HKPA). Only DAB, LP and HKPA were appointed to the Executive Council of CE Tung's first administration (Cheung, 2002; The Electoral System and Progress to Direct Elections https://publications.parliament.uk/pa/cm199798/cmselect/cmfaff/710/71004.htm).

21 These political parties included Democratic Party, Association for Democracy and People's Livelihood, the Frontier and the Citizen's Party (Kuan, 1999).

22 For instance, Andrew Cheng, a founding member of Democratic Party, moved a motion to request for direction election of all members of the LegCo in 2000 and the

CE in 2002. https://www.legco.gov.hk/yr98-99/english/counmtg/agenda/ord1507. htm#m_1

23 Interview with a former senior civil servant, 18 October 2010.

24 Minutes of Special Meeting, LegCo Panel on Administration of Justice and Legal Services (Papers) 23 March 1998. http://www.legco.gov.hk/yr97-98/english/panels/ ajls/minutes/aj230398.htm

25 Statement by the Secretary for Justice at the LegCo AJLS Panel. 4 February 1999; http://www.info.gov.hk/gia/general/199902/04/0204140.htm

26 LegCo Member's Motion, 10 March 1999. https://www.legco.gov.hk/yr98-99/ english/counmtg/agenda/ord1003.htm#m_2

27 According to the Functional Life Model, politicians and civil servants collaborate based on the need to ally against the external interference. See Chapter 1.

28 Hong Kong 1999–2000 Budget Speech. https://www.budget.gov.hk/1999/english/ bdgt1.htm#budget3

29 Rating and Evaluation Department, Private Domestic-Price Indices by Class (Territory-wide) https://www.rvd.gov.hk/en/property_market_statistics/index.html

30 Brief for the Legislative Council Civil Service Pay Adjustment. 2000. https://www. legco.gov.hk/yr99-00/english/panels/ps/papers/legcobrf.pdf

31 Legislative Council Panel on Public Service Meeting on 17 June 2002. https://www. csb.gov.hk/english/admin/csr/files/020607e.pdf

32 Legislative Council Panel on Public Service. https://www.csb.gov.hk/english/ admin/csr/files/020218.pdf

33 Emily Lau, the DP legislator, moved and passed a motion urging the Executive Authorities to conduct a public consultation the ministerial system, alongside the election of the CE and the LegCo by universal and equal suffrage. The Liberal Party legislator James Tien also supported examining the feasibility of a ministerial system, 12 January 2000. https://www.legco.gov.hk/yr99-00/english/counmtg/motion/ mot9900.htm

34 The Policy Address 2000. https://www.policyaddress.gov.hk/pa00/p54e.htm; Press Release Education Commission, 30 March 1999. https://www.info.gov.hk/gia/ general/199903/30/0330173.htm

35 Interview with a former senior civil servant, 8 January 2010.

36 Item for Establishment Subcommittee of Finance Committee; Head 21 – Chief Executive's Office https://www.legco.gov.hk/yr05-06/english/fc/esc/papers/e05-06e.pdf

37 Constitutional Affairs Bureaus. 26 October 2001. https://www.legco.gov.hk/yr01-02/english/panels/ca/papers/ca1030cb2-194-1.pdf

38 In the Executive Council of the first Tung administration, there were 11 non-official members and only three official members, including Chief Secretary, Financial Secretary and Secretary for Justice, very similar to the composite of ExCo since 1987 (Miners, 1998, p. 73). Hong Kong Yearbook 1997. https://www.yearbook.gov. hk/1997/ch2/e2f.htm

39 Interview with a former senior civil servant, 18 October 2010. The bracket is added by the author.

40 Interview with a former PO, 21 July 2009.

41 Comments. South China Morning Post, 20 April 2001.

References

Beijing Time (2001) *Full Text of Tung Chee Hwa's Re-Election Speech.* 14 December. http://en.people.cn/200112/13/eng20011213_86634.shtml

Burns, J. P. and Li, W. (2015) The Impact of External Change on Civil Service Values in Post-Colonial Hong Kong. *China Quarterly*, 222(June), pp. 522–546.

Chan, D. W. (2000) Vision, Task, and Hope: The Hong Kong Education Reform Movement in the 21st Century. *Educational Research Journal*, 15(1), pp. 1–18.

Cheung, A. B. L. (1997) Rebureaucratisation of Politics in Hong Kong: Prospects after 1997. *Asian Survey*, 37(8), pp. 720–737.

Cheung, A. B. L. (2002) 'The Changing Political System: Executive-led Government or 'Disabled' Governance.' In Lau, S.-k. (ed.) *The First Tung Chee-hwa Administration: The First Five Years of the Hong Kong Special Administration Region.* Hong Kong: The Chinese University Press, pp. 41–68.

Cliff, B. (2009) Outgoing Chief Prosecutor Sticks by His Decisions. *South China Morning Post*, 9 November.

Cooper, T. L. and Lui, T. L. (1990) Democracy and the Administrative State: The Case of Hong Kong. *Public Administration Review*, 50(3), pp. 332–344.

Dimbleby, J. (1997) *The Last Governor: Chris Pattern & the Handover of Hong Kong.* London: Warner Books.

Hong Kong Consumer Council (1996) *Competition Policy: The Key to Hong Kong's Future Economic Success.* https://www.consumer.org.hk/f/initiative_detail/301132/406997/competitionpolicy_report.pdf

Jao, Y. C. (2001) *The Asian Financial Crisis and the Ordeal of Hong Kong.* Westport, CT: Quorum Books.

King, A. Y.-c. (1975) Administrative Absorption of Politics in Hong Kong: Emphasis on the Grassroots Level. *Asian Survey*, 15(5), pp. 422–439.

Kuan, H.-c. (1999) 'Introduction.' In Kuan, H-c., Lau, S-k., Louie, K-s. and Wong, T. K-y. (eds.) *Power Transfer and Electoral Politics.* Hong Kong: The Chinese University Press, pp. 13–35.

Lau, S-k. (2002) 'Chronology.' In Lau S-k (ed.) *The First Tung Chee-hwa Administration: The First Five Years of the Hong Kong Special Administration Region.* Hong Kong: The Chinese University Press, pp. xi–xx.

Lee, A. Y. L. (1999) 'The Role of Newspapers in the 1967 Riot-A Case Study of the Partisanship of the Hong Kong Press.' In So, C. Y. K. and Chan, J. M. (eds.) *Press and Politics in Hong Kong-Case Studies from 1967 to 1997.* Hong Kong: Hong Kong Institute of Asia-Pacific Studies, The Chinese University of Hong Kong, pp. 33–66.

Legislative Council Commission (2021) History of the Legislative Council. https://www.legco.gov.hk/yr98-99/english/intro/hist_lc.htm. Accessed on 16 August 2021.

Lo, S-h. (1997) *The Politics of Democratisation in Hong Kong.* Houndmills, Hampshire: Macmillan Press; New York: St. Martin's Press.

Miners, N. (1998) *The Government and Politics of Hong Kong.* Hong Kong: Oxford University Press.

Ming Pao Press Editorial Committee (1996) *New Biography of Tung Chee Wah (董建华新传).* Hong Kong: Ming Pao Press.

Painter, M. (2005) Transforming the Administrative State: Reform in Hong Kong and the Future of the Developmental State. *Public Administration Review*, 65(3), pp. 335–346.

Qian, Q. (1997) National People's Congress Preparatory Committee of the Hong Kong SAR Working Report (全国人民代表大会香港特别行政区筹备委员会工作报告). http://www.gov.cn/test/2008-04/22/content_951279.htm. 10 March. *People's Daily.*

Scott, I. (2005) *Public Administration in Hong Kong: Regime Change and Its Impact on the Public Sector.* Singapore: Marshall Cavendish International.

Tsang, S. (2007) *Governing Hong Kong: Administrative Officers from the Nineteenth Century to the Handover to China. 1862–1997.* Hong Kong: Hong Kong University Press.

Tsang, W. K. (2006) Reform Hong Kong's Medium of Instruction in Secondary Schools: Review and Criticism (香港中学教学语言政策改革: 检讨与批判). *Education Journal(教育学报)*, 33, pp. 1–2.

Tung, C. H. (1996) Building a 21st Century Hong Kong Together (共同建设二十一世纪的香港). *Tai Kung Po (News of Hong Kong Section)* 29 October.

Xinhua News Agency (2018) *Biography of Tung Chee Wah (董建华简历)*. http://www.gov.cn/guoqing/2018-03/14/content_5274252.htm.

Yan, X. J. (2001) Mother-tongue Education in Hong Kong. *Pacific Neighbourhood Consortium*. http://140.109.14.50/annual/annual2001/hk%20pdf/jackie%20xiu%20yan.pdf

3 Reform impact
2002–2005

3.1 Social-economic-political contexts

Real GDP growth has moderately recovered from the dotcom bubble burst in 2000 when the first PO team appointed under the POAS started their tenure. However, the unemployment rate (7.3%) and budget deficits (HK$61.7 billion) remained high in 2002. In early 2003, SARS claimed 299 lives in Hong Kong and dealt a severe blow to its economy. However, this downturn only lasted for a few months and by May 2003, sectors such as tourism, local consumption and trade had recovered. The unemployment rate also stabilised after June 2003 (Siu and Wong, 2004).

Hong Kong's population increased rapidly from 1990 and had reached 6.71 million by 2002, representing an increase of over 1 million. Although property prices dropped after 1998, the shortage of housing remained. The population gradually aged from 1981 to 2006, with the percentage of those over 65 rising and those under 14 declining (Hong Kong Census and Statistics Department, 2007, p. 11). Immigrants arriving from mainland China under the one-way permit scheme aimed at reuniting families added 272,100 to the total population from 1997 to 2001, contributing 93% of the net local population growth during the period. The percentage of these immigrants in the total local population rose from 2.6% in 1991 to 4% in 2001 (Hong Kong Taskforce on Population Policy, 2003, p. 17).

By 2003, the education level of the Hong Kong population had increased dramatically. The percentage of those aged 15 and over who received tertiary education rose from 11.9% in 1992 to 20.5% in 2002 (Hong Kong Census and Statistics Department, 2003, p. 252). As a significant social-economic indicator, education predicted the voters' choice of the Democratic Party (DP) in the Legislative Council (LegCo) direct elections in 1998. The DP was regarded as a champion of democracy, and was in opposition to the government and China's Communist Party; those voting in the LegCo elections were relatively young and had received a high level of education, and were thus less satisfied with the progress of democratisation in Hong Kong. DP voters supported the implementation of a specific form of democracy, which they believed to be the

DOI: 10.4324/9781003195924-3

best political system for Hong Kong. They urged that (1) a Chief Executive (CE) should be directly elected as soon as possible and be subject to supervision by the LegCo and (2) functional constituencies should be returned by direct election (Kuan and Lau, 2002).

The Hong Kong population was divided in terms of their perceptions of local and national identities. A few years after the handover, a survey showed that the percentage of people who identified as both Hong Kongers and Chinese increased (Fung, 2004). However, the overall percentage remained below 50% from 1997 to 2002 and a larger percentage of those in the 18–29 age group perceived themselves exclusively as Hong Kongers (Hong Kong Public Opinion Research Institute, 2021). Nevertheless, in the 2000 election, the share of votes and constituency seats held by the pan-democrat political camp declined, whereas that of the pro-establishment political camp[1] increased (Wong, 2015, p. 7). The incomes of the DP and Civic Party (CP), the leading political parties, were reported to have declined, whereas that of the DAB, a leading pro-establishment party, increased rapidly (Wong, 2015, p. 107).

In this favourable social-economic-political context, the Tung administration should have had more room to implement major initiatives concerning the restructuring of the economy in the second term than in the first. However, the political team's lack of coordination and capacity and the adverse political-administrative relations somewhat limited the achievements of the Tung administration during this period.

3.2 Political-administrative relations under Tung administration (2002–2005)

The first Policy Address (Hong Kong Chief Executive, 2003) of the second term of Tung's administration stated that to restructure the economy after recovering from the recession, the Hong Kong SAR government should 'embark on important initiatives on a macro-level…include investing heavily in education, upgrading economic infrastructure, promoting innovation and technology, improving the business environment, helping the business sector to develop new markets, actively protecting our ecology and environment and improving our quality of life'. Despite setting these long-term goals, the Tung administration prioritised the short-term aim of reducing the fiscal deficit, which was regarded as being due to increases in welfare spending because of the economic downturn and an ageing population, the drop in revenue from land sales and related sources, the decline in tax revenues and the postponement of the second offering of Mass Transit Railway Corporation shares (Hong Kong Financial Secretary, 2003). Various reform measures aimed at privatising and downsizing the public sector were thus adopted, leading to extensive bureaucratic and sectoral conflicts. These conflicts, combined with the mismanagement of the SARs pandemic and the bad timing of implementing

Article 23 of the Basic Law concerning national security, helped to fuel the organisation of a mass demonstration by the various democratic political parties, which brought extensive international attention.

As discussed in Chapter 2, the POAS reform enabled Tung to recruit outsiders who supported his vision and agenda. However, among 14 Principal Officials nominated by Tung, 6 were career administrative officers (AOs) and the other outsiders had weak ties with grassroots communities and no experience of electoral politics (Table 3.1). They were also divided along ideological lines. Some were left-oriented and believed in big government and social-economic equality, whereas others were right-oriented and believed in the free market and small government. Insider POs (former AOs) shared beliefs concerning incremental policy change or short-term firefighting, to guard against administrative mistakes and political risks.

One outsider PO complained that civil servants lacked any long-term strategy:

> They [civil servants] love doing it issue by issue. It's typical colonial government [style]. Things change along the way, that's fine. You just accommodate changes or make amendments to original strategy. But without that, you would be three blind mice hitting each other and you just do firefighting. Every time something comes out, you scramble something together.[2]

Another outsider PO identified institutional factors that prevented civil servants from proactively making changes that could be risky:

> For civil servants, particularly in our system, if you do 10 tasks, even you did 9 of them beautifully, nobody will praise you because you are expected to do well. Even if only one of them had any problems, you will be criticised by the LegCo. The LegCo members would demand your resignation, accountability or all kinds of things. The media will criticise you. At the minimum, the promotion of civil servants would be affected. So why make any changes?[3]

An outsider PO also complained that the political team lacked a coherent political ideology to guide their initiatives:

> We were given some brainstorming sessions by the CH [Tung]. They were not really political philosophies. One of my earlier complaints was that we don't have unifying philosophies to govern us. If we have unifying philosophies, if I agree with them, I can stay in the government. If I don't agree with them, I shouldn't be in the government. And we don't have that. So, you have some people who are terribly right wing, and somebody very left wing.[4]

Table 3.1 Principal officials (policy secretaries) of HKSARG in July 2002

Position titles in July 2002	Background	Political party affiliation before taking the position
Chief Secretary for Administration (CSA)	A career AO in HKSARG	Nil
Financial Secretary (FS)	Investment bank senior manager	Nil
Secretary for Justice (SJ)	A private solicitor and law firm partner	A founding member of DAB
Secretary for the Civil Service	A career AO in HKSARG	Nil
Secretary for Commerce, Industry and Technology	industrialist	LP
Secretary for Constitutional Affairs	A career AO in HKSARG	Nil
Secretary for Economic Development and Labour	A career AO in HKSARG	Nil
Secretary for Education	A medical professional and university manager	Nil
Secretary for Environment, Transport and Works	An engineer and founder of an environmental consulting firm	Nil
Secretary for Financial Services and the Treasury	A financial manager in the private sector	Nil
Secretary for Home Affairs	A medical professional	Nil
Secretary for Housing, Planning and Lands	A career AO in HKSARG	Nil
Secretary for Security	A career AO in HKARG	Nil
Secretary for Health, Welfare and Food	A medical professional	Nil

Source: Beijing Times, 'New Team of Hong Kong Principal Officials Appointed' 25 June 2002; China Vitae; Personal websites.

The contrasting styles of proactive and risk-taking POs, particularly those of outsiders, and reactive and risk-averse senior civil servants, at times resulted in adversarial political-administrative relations in policymaking.

3.2.1   *Explaining adversarial political-administrative relations*

3.2.1.1   *Case 3.1: Electronic Road Pricing*

The government conducted a feasibility study of Electronic Road Pricing (ERP) in 1997, aimed at tackling the traffic congestion and air pollution problems in Hong Kong that had resulted from the sharp increase in private vehicles in some areas. They made the decision not to implement ERP in 2001, given that the speed of traffic was forecast to rise by 2011 and alternative measures could be taken to reduce private car use and vehicle emissions (Transport Bureau, 2001). The career AO Siu Kwing-chue was the Secretary for Transport at this time. After the external environmental consultant Ms Liao Sau-Tung (Liao) became the Secretary for the Environment, Transport and Works, she openly advocated for re-examining ERP as an option in 2003. However, in a media interview, Liao revealed that a senior civil servant in the bureau had *'repeatedly warned her'* that ERP was untouchable because of the political risks involved (South China Morning Post, 2007). ERP was also opposed by some LegCo members.[5] However, Liao was supported by the Transport Department and various environmental groups,[6] and managed to put ERP on the bureau's agenda in 2006 (Legislative Council, 2006) and on the consultation agenda of the Council for Sustainable Development in 2007.[7]

This case reveals how an outsider PO overruled the bureau civil servants' objections and initiated a controversial policy change. As an environmental engineer, she had the technical capability to initiate ERP, but also enjoyed the support of the environmental community. The Expanded Principal-Agent Model suggests that the political-administrative relationship in Case I is an 'advocacy coalition' between politicians and bureaucrats in terms of information, although they have conflicting goals.

This case confirms H2 and H3b, and the following hypothesis is proposed:

Under the structural role differentiation between political appointees and civil servants, the political-administrative relations in policymaking are likely to be adversarial when 1) political appointees and civil servants have different career and professional backgrounds; 2) political appointees have technical capability to initiate the issues; and 3) the public mood is intensive and critical of the government.

Civil servants can resist policy initiatives by remaining silent about implementation problems in the policy formulation stage or not engaging in their implementation if political appointees have limited knowledge of sectoral conflicts. The Expanded Principal-Agent Model indicates that such political-administrative relations in policymaking are principal-agent types. The policy bureaus and departments of Hong Kong are structurally separate. The bureau civil servants are generalists and responsible for formulating policies and overseeing their implementation, whereas most departmental civil servants are professionals and responsible for implementing policy, which often involves mediation between sectors. Outsider POs have many issues to attend to and limited knowledge of sectoral politics, and thus must rely on the bureau civil servants to anticipate implementation problems and issues with interest groups and address these alongside their department colleagues in the policy formulation stage. When working relations between an outsider PO and the permanent secretary lack trust and cooperation fails, the implementation of policies is likely to involve sectoral resistance and conflict.

For example, after an outsider PO rushed to publicly announce a policy change that affected the departmental client groups, one civil servant in the department complained, '*Civil servants would not like it because we have been doing this for 15 years. You don't disturb the card here. When you came just five days, proposed to change this...*'.[8]

3.2.1.2 Case 3.2: Construction and demolition waste charging scheme

The government introduced a charging scheme regulation in May 1995 to provide economic incentives to reduce construction and demolition waste, but this was opposed by waste haulers due to various concerns, such as payment methods and debt issues. The waste trade associations staged a landfill blockade to protest against the scheme in June 1996. The government then agreed to suspend the implementation of the scheme. It took six years of negotiation and numerous LegCo panel discussions before the government again proposed a waste charging scheme to the LegCo in May 2002, before the politically appointed PO team started their term.

Ms Liao Sau-Tung, an outsider PO, supported the scheme but had limited knowledge of the waste haulers' previous opposition and the implementation problems. A few days after the charging scheme was implemented, on 26 January 2006, a blockade of three landfills by over 100 construction waste trucks took place. The protest was against the categorisation of recyclable versus non-recyclable waste and the weighing method (Yung, 2006). The drivers, the Department of Environmental Protection and the Department of Civil Engineering and Development held initial negotiations but did not reach a consensus (Oriental Daily, 2006). Liao then had to personally negotiate with driver representatives and agreed to be more flexible in the categorisations of waste and the weighing, in addition to simplifying the administrative procedures of waste charging.[9]

This case illustrates that the outsider PO was not adequately advised and supported by senior civil servants in the bureau, and thus the charging scheme was not smoothly implemented. Under the Expanded Principal-Agent Model, the political-administrative policymaking relations represented a principal-agent relationship, because the outsider PO knew little about the politics of the situation, and although the senior civil servants had the information, they chose to withhold it from the PO. The civil servants in the bureau can be categorised as classical bureaucrats, as in Image I, as they are reactive in their programme commitment and have a low tolerance of politics.

Case 3.2 Confirms H2 and H3b, and the following hypothesis is proposed:

Under the structural role differentiation between political appointees and civil servants, the political-administrative relations in policymaking are likely to be adversarial when 1) political appointees and civil servants have different career and professional backgrounds; 2) the policy initiation has risk of invoking public criticism; and 3) the public mood is intensive.

3.2.2   Explaining collaborative political-administrative relations

3.2.2.1   Case 3.3: Reforming senior secondary school education

In 2000, the Education Commission published a reform proposal at the request of CE Tung. The proposal suggested reforming secondary school education to make it more diverse and flexible, which can prepare students for life-long learning and employability (Education Commission, 2000). The proposal was implemented in 2001, but concerns were raised by the school sector and communities, who felt that the diversification of the curriculum and student evaluation created too great a workload for teachers (Legislative Council, 2004a). The outsider PO Professor Li Kwok-cheung (Li) joined the government in 2002 and collaborated with permanent secretary Law Fan Chiu-fun (Law), who was the Secretary for Education before Li, to formulate and implement the reform measures. Their backgrounds partly explained their commitment to the reform. Li was a former university manager who believed in education equality and diversity and was critical of the government's education policy (Li, 2005). Although Law was a career AO, she had a passion for educational reform and strongly believed that it was necessary.[10] The resistance from the education department was also reduced after it was merged with the education bureau, and this enabled Li and Law to push forward the reform implementation despite criticism from stakeholders in the school sector.

The collaborative relations between the PO and senior civil servant in this case are similar to the functional village life model, in which two parties share goals and values. The Expanded Principal-Agent Model also suggests that this relationship is like a policy subsystem, in which both politicians and bureaucrats have extensive information about the policy and reach a consensus about the goals.

Case 3.3 confirms H2, but not H3b or H4d. Based on Case 3.3, the following hypothesis is proposed:

> Under the structural role differentiation between political appointees and civil servants, the political-administrative relations in policymaking are likely to be collaborative when 1) political appointees and civil servants have different career and professional backgrounds; 2) when political appointees and the civil servants share policy goals; and 3) the public mood is intensive.

3.2.2.2   Case 3.4: Home ownership policy change

CE Tung's first administration aimed to increase the rate of homeownership when high private housing prices were perceived to be creating extensive social and political problems. With the increased provision of subsidised housing units, the average waiting time for public rental housing was reduced from over six years in 1997 to less than three years in 2002 (Government Press Release, 2002a).

After the Asian financial crisis and the 40%–60% drop in housing prices in 1998, the government began to change its policy objectives. For example, its subsidised Sandwich Class Housing Scheme for those on middle incomes was abolished in 1999 (Chiu, 2002).

Mr Suen Ming-yeung (Suen), a career AO, was appointed the Secretary for Housing, Planning and Lands at the beginning of the Tung administration's second term. Suen announced nine measures to revive the property market, and in his statement he linked its prosperity to economic development. His aim was to restrict the government's role so it would *'principally focus on land supply and provision of rental assistance…withdraw as far as possible from other housing assistance programmes to minimise intervention in the market'*. The long-term target of achieving a rate of 70% home ownership in the population by 2007 was scrapped, and the production and sale of flats under the subsidised home ownership scheme (HOS) would permanently cease from 2003 (Government Press Release, 2002a). Although some senior civil servants had concerns about the drastic change regarding the HOS,[11] they were cooperative when it came to its implementation. For example, the proposal to dispose of the remaining HOS flats by selling them to private developers was supported by civil servants. This generated immediate revenue for the government, although the risk of being perceived as favouring private developers was acknowledged (LegCo Select Committee, 2010, p. 153). The public was generally supportive of the policy change, as were legislators of different political camps (Legislative Council, 2002), although it reduced the supply of housing units for future middle- and lower-income groups and was not a sustainable approach to curbing housing price rises during economic upturns.

In Case 3.4, the insider PO and senior civil servants had a collaborative working relationship. From the perspective of the Image IV model, the insider PO was a 'traditional personnel' taking up a novel role, and the political aspect of his former AO position was enhanced. The senior civil servants were involved in the policymaking and had a high tolerance of private-interest politics, but their commitment to government-subsidised housing programmes was low. They can be characterised as traditional bureaucrats.

Case 3.4, therefore, confirms H2, H3a and H4a. The following hypothesis is proposed:

> Under the structural role differentiation between political appointees and civil servants, the political-administrative relations in policymaking are likely to be collaborative when 1) political appointees and civil servants have similar career backgrounds; and 2) the public mood is intensive and generally supportive of the government.

3.2.2.3   Case 3.5: The National Security Bill

Under the POAS, more POs were appointed by the Central People's Government (CPG), which could directly influence the policy agenda. Article 23 of the Basic Law was one example, which triggered street protests involving hundreds of thousands people on 1 July 2003.

Article 23 stipulates the following:

> The Hong Kong Special Administrative Region shall enact laws on its own to prohibit any act of treason, secession, sedition, subversion against the Central People's Government, or theft of state secrets, to prohibit foreign political organisations or bodies from conducting political activities in the Region, and to prohibit political organisations or bodies of the Region from establishing ties with foreign political organisations or bodies.

Relations between the CPG and the Hong Kong SAR in terms of protecting national security were central to the Article, which was first formulated in the late 1980s.[12] The Hong Kong side was concerned that freedom of expression would be prohibited if the Article adopted broad definitions of treason, secession, sedition and subversion, while the CPG side was concerned that local political organisations could engage foreign political forces, which would threaten domestic stability and national unity. A compromise was reached, and in the final version of Article 23, broad terms, such as 'causing' either a breach of national unity or subversion of the CPG, were removed, which enabled Hong Kong to enact relevant laws locally (Li, 2012, pp. 192–197).

The CPG's official Vice-Premier Qian Qichen (Qian) and the National People's Congress Vice-Director of the Legislation Work Committee Qiao Xiaoyang urged the Hong Kong government to legislate Article 23 in June 2002, immediately before the inauguration of the second administration under Tung. Qian expressed concerns that organisations such as Fa Lun Gong, an illegal religious group based in mainland China, might liaise with organisations in foreign countries via Hong Kong and engage in illegal activities (against China). However, he also expressed his hope that local legislation would be supported by the majority of local people through discussion (Sing Pao Daily News, 2002).

The agenda of legislating Article 23 was set by the CPG, but the legislation was delegated to local government. Therefore, the type of Public Service Bargain is a delegated agency bargain (Hood and Lodge, 2006, pp. 42–60). Two POs were in charge of the legislation process: the Secretary for Justice, who was an outsider PO trusted by the CPG, and the Secretary for Security, an insider PO with an AO career. The public consultation document was issued by the Security Bureau because it was trusted to possess the professional judgement to protect the nation's sovereignty, unity and territorial integrity. The document addressed the CPG's concerns about Fa Lung Gong by proposing to

> make it an offence to organise or support activities of an organisation proscribed in the interests of national security, especially if the organisation is affiliated with a Mainland organisation which has been proscribed by the CPG on the grounds that it endangers national security.
>
> (Government Press Release, 2002b)

Opposing legislators, legal professionals, journalists, rights-based NGOs, academics and religious groups had various concerns about the wording in the bill. These included the broad and ambiguous definitions of criminal liabilities, such as treason, sedition, subversion and secession; the definitions of political organisations or bodies and protected information; the extended investigative powers of the police; the suppression of the freedom of expression, the press and association and the protection of human rights; and the lack of sufficient detail in the bill and time for public consultation (Legislative Council, 2003c).

The National Security (Legislative Provisions) Bill (the Bill) submitted to the LegCo on 14 February 2003 made some concessions that addressed these concerns: abolishing offences of the misprision of treason and the possession of seditious publications; narrowing the definitions of secession and subversion offences and of 'unauthorised access to protected information'; restricting the power to proscribe a local organisation and of investigation; limiting the application of the offence of treason; and stating that appeals by proscribed organisations will be adjudicated by courts instead of a tribunal (Legislative Council, 2003d; Security Bureau, 2003). However, the opposing camp was not satisfied and requested that a white paper be published for public consultation.

The government counted on the votes of the DAB and the Liberal Party to pass the Bill. Some legislators and political and religious organisations appealed for people to attend a rally to oppose the Bill on 1 July 2003. The local economy was hit hard by the SARS epidemic and the public was dissatisfied with the government's performance at the time (Cheung, 2004). Hundreds of thousands of people attended the protest, and the Liberal Party Chair announced they would propose a motion to adjourn the Bill on 5 July 2003. The CE announced on the same day that the Executive Council had agreed to address the community's concerns and make further amendments to the Bill, including removing the provision regarding proscribing a local organisation subordinate of a mainland organisation that had been initially proscribed by the CPG (Government Press Release, 2003a). Hu Jintao also replaced Jiang Zeming as the president of the CPG at this time. However, the CE's concession did not win over the support of the Liberal Party, and the Bill was deferred (Peterson, 2005).

In this case, the PO and senior civil servants were in a collaborative relationship.[13] However, the high level of political conflicts associated with the local identity politics could not be effectively managed and reduced by the local administration alone.

Case 3.5 confirms H2, H3a and H4, and the following hypothesis is proposed:

> Under the structural role differentiation between political appointees and civil servants, the political-administrative relations in policymaking are likely to be collaborative when 1) the issue is new with no proved solutions; 2) political appointees and civil servants have similar career backgrounds; 3) the public mood is intensive and critical of the government; and 4) the political appointee initiate unpopular policies mandated by a superior jurisdiction.

3.2.3   Explaining mutually respectful political-administrative relations

Case 3.6: Authorising betting on football

A policy committee consisting of civil servants proposed before 2002 that football betting should be authorised. This was an amendment to the long-established gambling policy aimed at restricting gambling opportunities to a limited number of authorised and regulated outlets (Legislative Council Brief, 2001). The government issued a Consultation Paper on the Gambling Review in 2001 and set the regulatory framework that imposes licencing conditions such as forbidding underage and credit-based gambling and restricting the provision of excessive gambling opportunities and promotional activities. With the support of the Liberal Party and gambling operators such as the Jockey Club (Legislative Council, 2003a), senior civil servants led the lobbying of the LegCo and interest groups. The consultation was completed after the outsider PO became the Secretary for Home Affairs (SHA) under the POAS, and supported the decision to authorise football betting (Government Press Release, 2002c). The then Permanent Secretary Lee Lai-kuen believed that her lobbying regarding this bill was successful partly because of her trusting relations with legislators in opposing political camps, which she developed through her earlier work experience in the LegCo (East Week, 2009).

In this case, the working relationships between the outsider PO and senior civil servants were mutually respectful. Although the policy was already formulated when the outsider PO joined the government, he trusted and supported the civil servants. Such trust could be risky to the PO, given the adverse political environment surrounding the Bill itself[14] and the government in general.[15] The mutual respect and trust between Ho and Lee were said to be attributable to their educational backgrounds: both were from elite schools and were in the same music class at school [16].

The support from the political team was a critical factor as the bill was a high priority for the government. A reduction in welfare expenditure was planned at the time, to balance the budget deficit, and the government was looking for alternative methods of providing local charities with financial support. Authorising football betting would generate tax revenues that could be directed towards the charities (Deans, 2003).

In Case 3.6, the senior civil servants were similar to the political bureaucrats in Image IV, as they were tolerant of politics and had commitment to policy programmes. The Expanded Principal-Agent Model indicates that such political-administrative relations are characteristic of a 'bottom line', in which bureaucrats dominate the policy area through their expertise and share goals with their political principals. However, civil servants in this case were not like those bureaucrats who had technical expertise but were passive (Waterman and Meier, 1998, p. 192). Instead, the civil servants proactively pushed forward their pet policies with the support of the political team.

Case 3.6 confirms H2, H3a and H4, and the following hypothesis is then proposed:

> Under the structural role differentiation between political appointees and civil servants, their working relations in policymaking are likely to be mutually respectful when 1) political appointees and civil servants have similar educational backgrounds; 2) political appointees have technical capability of handling the issue; 3) there is support from the whole political team; and 4) the public mood is intensive and critical of the government.

3.3 Contesting Public Service Bargains amidst adversarial political environment

3.3.1 *Divisive personnel management reforms in the public sector*

In addition to the structural role change of senior civil servants under the POAS, reforms that downsized the civil service, reduced civil service pay and privatised public services intensified the conflicts inside the government and destabilised the agency bargain developed after the POAS (Table 3.2). These reform measures were partly aimed at achieving the target of reducing the operating expenditure of government departments and agencies by 5% between 1999 and 2002 (Finance Bureau, 1999).

Table 3.2 Major civil service reform measures under the Tung administration

Date	Event	Scope
January 1999	CE announcement in LegCo	Introduce the Enhanced Productivity Programme; Reform the civil service to enhance its efficiency
March 1999	Consultation document published	Review entry and exit mechanisms, pay and fringe benefits, disciplinary procedures, performance management, professional training and personnel development
1999	Introduced non-civil service contract (NCSC) staff scheme	Provide a flexible means of employing staff on fixed term contracts outside the civil service establishment, to meet short-term, part-time and seasonal service needs
April 2000	Introduced new disciplinary mechanism	Set up a new independent secretariat to centrally process formal disciplinary cases and streamline the disciplinary procedures
June 2000	Introduced the new entry system	Most recruits were initially appointed on probationary or agreement terms before being considered for permanent appointment
	Introduced civil service provident fund scheme	To replace the non-contribution pension system with a mandatory and voluntary contribution fund scheme
	Introduced a new fringe benefits package	Revise leave packages and reduce allowances to reduce expenditure
July 2000	introduced the first voluntary retirement scheme	9,800 existing staff retired voluntarily with pension benefits and compensation
September 2000	introduced a Management-Initiated Retirement Scheme	To provide for retirement of directorate civil servants to facilitate Government re-organisation
October 2000	Introduced elements of performance-based reward systems into the civil service	Adopted (1) target-based assessment and core competencies assessment and (2) assessment panels for performance appraisal
March 2003	Introduced the second voluntary retirement scheme	Voluntary retirement of 5,300 staff with pension benefits and compensation

Source: Civil Service Reform Summary (Hong Kong Civil Service Bureau https://www.csb.gov.hk/english/admin/csr/9.html.); Civil Service Reform Consultation Document (Hong Kong Civil Service Bureau, March 1999. https://www.info.gov.hk/archive/consult/1999/reforme.pdf).

The reform reduced the civil service staff levels from 198,000 in January 2000 to about 161,000 by March 2007. The Public Officer Pay Adjustment Ordinance enacted in July 2002 to enable the civil service pay cuts was challenged by judicial reviews submitted by police officers, police associations, civil service unions, expatriate civil servants and a legal officer. The Public Officer Pay Adjustment (2004/2005) was passed by the LegCo in 2003, a legal officer challenged whether it was consistent with Article 103 of the Basic Law and the Court of First Instance ruled in favour of his challenge (Hong Kong Court of Appeal, 2004). In 2005, the government appealed against the judgement and the Court of Final Appeal ruled in favour of the government (Xinhua, 2005).

Civil service unions opposing the reform also made submissions to the Hong Kong government (Civil Service Bureau, 2003) and expressed their concerns about the pay adjustment to officials of the CPG (Hong Kong Economic Times, 2004). Legislators from the Liberal Party supported the reform to reduce fiscal deficits, whereas those with union backgrounds[17] from various political camps opposed it (Legislative Council, 2004b).

The NCSC staff scheme enabled the government to meet the civil service reduction target and reduce the expenditure on personnel, as those employed under the scheme enjoyed less-favourable benefits as civil servants. The scheme also enabled individual bureaus and departments to manage their personnel more flexibly. However, most NCSC staff received low salaries and were non-skilled. By December 2005, of the 15,687 NCSC staff employed, nearly 78% received a monthly salary of between HK$8,000 and HK$15,999, whereas the starting pay point of the Directorate Pay Scale for senior civil servants was HK$92,650 as of January 2005. In addition, about 40% of NCSC staff had continuously been in service for over 3 years rather than serving 'temporarily' or 'seasonally' (Legislative Council, 2003b, 2005a). One former senior civil servant confirmed that administrative staff were hired under the staff scheme to achieve the department's savings targets.[18]

These less-favourable employment conditions for NCSC staff widened the income gap within the government and were criticised by legislators with union backgrounds from different political camps as being unsustainable and contradicting the goal of promoting overall employment (Legislative Council, 2005b).

The statutory bodies that were heavily funded by the government also underwent personnel management reforms similar to those of the civil service. These were also aimed at reducing expenditure by 5% under the Enhanced Productivity Programme. For example, the Hospital Authority (HA), the largest statutory body to provide public health care in Hong Kong, received over 90% of its income from recurrent government subvention (Hospital Authority, 2001). By December 2001, the HA managed 44 public hospitals and institutions, 49 specialist outpatient clinics and 13 general outpatient clinics (Hospital Authority, 2002). The HA's staff management policy followed the principle of cost comparability with the civil service. Following the government reform measures, the HA reduced the entry-level starting salaries of new recruits and serving staff on in-service appointments in 2000. Annual pay increments were also linked to performance, allowance and expenses/ reimbursements were abolished and the contract-based employment of medical trainees and medical officers increased, partly due to fiscal constraints (Legislative Council, 2005c).

The reform resulted in feelings of inequity and concerns about job security in new recruits and junior staff. In addition, senior managers such as the CE, the Cluster CEs and the Hospital CE of the HA received 30% and 15% of their basic salaries and cash allowances during the 1998–2002 period, respectively (Legislative Council, 2004c). The reform thus increased the tension between the management and unionised frontline staff within the HA. The HA management was criticised as being incompetent in its response to the community outbreak of the deadly SARS epidemic, due to its lack of coordination with regional Department of Health offices and the private sector, and in its communications with staff, patients and the local population (SARS Expert Committee, 2003). The reform was not in step with the increasing health care demand brought by the ageing population. This, along with the shortage of manpower, led to an increased turnover rate of doctors from below 3% before 2002/03 to over 6% in 2006/07 (Hospital Authority, 2008).

Senior executives of some statutory bodies were also criticised for being paid much higher salaries than senior government officials (Scott, 2006). Following the passage of a motion in the LegCo in 2001, the government commissioned a consultancy study to review the compensation awarded to the top three-tier executives in 10 statutory bodies, which received over 50% of their operation income from government subvention (Scott, 2006). Most of the statutory bodies being reviewed accepted the recommendations and adjusted the pay structure according to the trends in the sector, and became more transparent in disclosing senior executives' remuneration (Hong Kong Government Administrative Wing, 2003).

These divisive personnel management reforms were thus a major source of political-administrative conflict within the executive government. As one outsider PO admitted, the reform 'upsets everybody, not just through salary cuts, but by making them (public officials) more accountable'.[19]

3.3.2   *Politics of blames between politicians and bureaucrats*

3.3.2.1   *Case 3.7: Sponsoring Harbour Fest*

Harbour Fest (HF) was a publicity and promotion event that received HK$100 million in government funding and was aimed at reviving the economy after the SARS epidemic. The event was proposed by the American Chamber of Commerce (AmCham) in Hong Kong, whose chairman was a non-official member of an advisory body chaired by the Financial Secretary (FS) with the aim of relaunching the economy. A high-level inter-bureau coordination group (Economic Relaunch Working Group, ERWG) chaired by the FS who was an outsider decided to sponsor the event and delegated its implementation to AmCham.[20] The organisations in this co-production approach became embroiled in blame politics when HF received extensive public criticism as unsuccessful. The department head (Director General of Investment Promotion; DGIP) was the Controlling Officer and was subject to disciplinary charges after being criticised by the Audit Report and the LegCo Public Accounts Committee Report investigating the decision and management processes of HF. By then, the FS role was taken up by another outsider PO, who believed that it was the DGIP's hands-off approach to implementation that led to the failure of HF. The DGIP insisted that his monitoring approach was consistent with the ERWG's decision that the government should sponsor HF but not get involved in its implementation.[21] The conflicts resulted in a successful judicial review by the former DGIP, and the disciplinary ruling against him was quashed.[22]

In this case, both outsider POs and the senior civil servant lacked experience, and no clear rules could be followed when monitoring the delivery of this mega event under the sponsorship of the government. In this highly antagonistic political environment, the politicians and bureaucrats blamed each other, leading to conflict in their working relationship.

Based on Case 3.7, H2, H3b and H4c are confirmed, and the following hypothesis is proposed:

Under the structural role differentiation between political appointees and civil servants, the political-administrative relations in policymaking are likely to be adversarial when 1) political appointees and civil servants have different career backgrounds; 2) the issue is under the purview of multiple political appointees, and the lead political appointee finds it difficult to control the subordinate civil servant; and 3) the public mood is intensive and critical of the government.

3.3.2.2   Case 3.8: Containing the SARS epidemic (I, II)

From November 2002 to August 2003, SARS, or Severe Acute Respiratory Syndrome, which was a relatively unknown disease at the time, emerged from southern Chinese provinces and infected around 8,422 people worldwide claiming 916 lives, representing a death rate of around 11%. Hong Kong was one of the hardest hit cities: 1,755 people became infected and 299 died. SARS in Hong Kong also gave rise to an adversarial political-administrative relationship: the outsider PO Secretary for Health Welfare and Food (SHWF), a medical doctor and public health manager, took responsibility for the unfortunate outcome of the pandemic and resigned. When SARs first spread in Hong Kong the SHWF was directly involved in disease control and initiated a contact-tracing e-system to monitor the situation.[23] However, as the pandemic became more serious, the SHWF supported the CE's preference of imposing draconian quarantine measures, but this initially met with resistance from the Director of Health, who withheld her knowledge and statutory authority to implement disease control measures, such as quarantining of contacts, entry and exit restrictions and isolating infected people or places.[24] The SHWF did get administrative support to coordinate inter-departmental responses to emergency situations from the Permanent Secretary for Welfare and Food.[25]

The relationship between the outsider PO and the departmental civil servant in this case evolved from the village life model to being conflicting when SARS became more serious and the political pressure to impose more stringent control measures increased. By contrast, the working relationship between the outsider PO and the senior civil servant in the bureau was collaborative as they had a common goal and a clear division of labour when responding to the emergency. The outsider PO SHWF did not shift blame onto the civil servants, but resigned from office after implementing the recommendations of the expert committee, which could better prepare the government for future outbreaks of infectious diseases. In his resignation letter, SHWF explicitly stated that he resigned to 'demonstrate political accountability and to bring a closure to this painful episode' (South China Morning Post, 2004).

Based on Case 3.8, H2 and H3a are confirmed and H4a and H4b are partially confirmed, but H4d is not. The following hypotheses are therefore proposed:

1) under the structural role differentiation between political appointees and civil servants, the political-administrative relations in policymaking are likely to be adversarial when 1) the public mood is critical of the government; 2) the issue is new with no proven solutions; 3) the political appointees have technical capabilities and attempt to control policymaking; and 4) political appointees and civil servants have similar professional backgrounds.

2) under the structural role differentiation between political appointees and civil servants, the political-administrative relations in policymaking are likely to be collaborative when 1) the political appointees and civil servants share policy goals; and 2) public mood is intensive and critical of the government.

3.4   Evaluating the POAS reform and its feedback

The POAS reform brought in many outsider POs who introduced new ideas and initiatives to the government. Although some had adversarial working relations with senior civil servants in terms of policymaking, they were viewed as possessing leadership qualities and as being more innovative than some senior civil servants.[26] The POAS also opened up opportunities for senior civil servants, particularly those at the AO level, to work in a political position. These 'insiders' were considered to have the ability to learn quickly and to be skilled at policy implementation. The structural role as a political appointee also changed these insiders' motives and behaviour. Although they were former civil servants, they became more sensitive to political demands under the POAS.[27]

Three POs (two outsiders and one insider) tendered their resignations before they completed the term. In addition to the SHWF, the FS apologised after being criticised for purchasing a new car just before he made the decision to raise taxes on such cars. He intended to resign but initially withdrew his resignation letter after being persuaded to stay by the CE. However, his resignation was finally accepted on 16 July 2003, amidst hostile criticism by some legislators and when the media reported the controversy (Government Press Release, 2003b; Legislative Council, 2003e). Like SHWF, FS explicitly expressed his political accountability in his resignation letter: '*I fully accept the formal criticism from the Chief Executive. I fully accept his conclusion that what I have done amounts to gross negligence and have clearly breached parts of the Code for Principal Officials under the Accountability System*' (Government Press Release, 2003c). In addition, the Secretary for Security, who led the formulation of the National Security Bill, tendered her resignation due to personal reasons a few days before the 1 July rally in protest of the Bill (News.gov.hk, 2003).

The fact that two POs left their offices prematurely and took political responsibility demonstrates the institutionalisation of the POAS reform. However, the precedents of losing reputation and positions deterred both 'outsiders' and 'insiders' from joining the PO team. A former Executive Councilor commented the following in an interview, when discussing the recruitment of capable outsiders to be POs during both the Tung and Tsang administrations:

People had politely declined and when they declined, they didn't give the real reasons, I'm sure…It's the 'heated kitchen'; the unclear policy and political environment in which people may or may not leave and jump back into the private sector.

Attracting competent civil servants to be POs also became harder:

We are even losing promising rising stars in the civil service…If you are a 40-something-year-old upcoming AO, then you know you should become one of these political appointees. Before you are too old, you jump…They have left the government and many of them have become heads of statutory bodies, a similar kind of job, very secure, so on and so forth, but you don't have to put up with this political constraint.[28]

Under the POAS, there was pressure to functionally politicise the civil service, making it responsive to the government of the day by 'integrating politically relevant aspects in the day-to-day functions' (Hustedt and Salomonsen, 2014). The unresponsiveness of senior civil servants is partly due to their legal obligations as Controlling Officers, reflecting a tension between responsive and responsible competency senior civil servants are required to have (Shaw and Eichbaum, 2020). They must ensure the safety, economy and advantages of public funds and government property. The Code for Principal Officials under the Accountability System also requires them to uphold the political neutrality of civil servants. However, 'political neutrality' is not defined in the Code (Chief Executive's Office, 2002). To strengthen responsive staff support for the POs to conduct political work, and to preserve the responsible competency and values of political neutrality of the civil service, the second CE introduced junior political appointees (political advisors) under the Political Appointment System (see Chapter 4).

The failure to legislate Article 23 of the Basic Law, the mass demonstration on 1 July 2003 and the resignation of three POs frustrated the CPG. The particularly high levels of social-economic-political conflicts and governance challenges during the period drove the CPG to proactively integrate Hong Kong's economic development with the regional development in mainland China (see Chapter 4).

Notes

1 The composition of the pan-democratic and pro-establishment political camps varied over the years. Wong (2015, p. 109) included in the former the 'Association for Democracy and People's Livelihood (ADPL) the Civic Act-Up, the Civic Party (CP), the Hong Kong Confederation of Trade Unions (CTU), the Citizen's Party, the Democratic Party (DP), the Frontier, the League of Social Democrats (LSD), the Neo Democrats (ND), the Neighborhood and Workers Service Centre (NWSC), and People Power (PP)'. Wong's book included in the latter 'Democratic Alliance for the Betterment and Progress of Hong Kong (DAB), the Hong Kong Federation of Trade Unions (FTU), and the Hong Kong Progressive Alliance (HKPA), Civil Force, the Liberal Party (LP), the New People's Party (NPP)'.

2 Interview with a former PO, 3 August 2009.

3 Interview with a former PO, 1 September 2009.

4 Interview with a former PO, 28 August 2009.

5 For example, Raymond Ho Chung-tai, the Legislative Councilor representing the engineering functional constituency, opposed the ERP. Minutes of special meeting, Legislative Council Panel on Planning, Lands and Works, 26 June 2006. LC Paper No. CB(1)60/06-07.

6 For example, the Civic Exchange supported introducing ERP. Metropolis Daily, 24 January 2007.

7 Clean Air-Clear Choice. Invitation and Response Document. https://www.enb.gov. hk/sites/default/files/susdev/html/en/council/baq_ird_e.pdf

8 Interview with a former senior civil servant, 3 September 2009.

9 Government Press Release. The Secretary for Environment, Transport and Works replied to journalists. 27 January 2006.

10 For example, to become fully informed before reforming the education system, Law studied for a Master of Education degree at a local university (Hong Kong Economic Journal Monthly, 2008).

11 Interview with a former civil servant, 7 May 2010.

12 While this Article was being discussed, the 4 June incident occurred, in which the Central government pacified the Tian'anmen Square protests by military force. This

incident affected the Hong Kong people's evaluation of the local political system (Lee, 2012).

13 This was confirmed by a PO and a senior civil servant who were involved in handling Article 23 legislation, through private interviews conducted in July and October 2009, respectively.

14 The bill was opposed by some religious, education and social service sector groups, along with legislators from the pan-democrat camp (Legislative Council, 2003a).

15 The authorising took effect in July 2003 when tens of thousands of people protested against the government's national security bill in Hong Kong.

16 Interview with a former senior official, 8 January 2010.

17 Wong Kwok-hing from the Hong Kong Federation of Trade Unions and Lee Cheuk-Yan from the Hong Kong Confederation of Trade Unions.

18 Interview with a former senior civil servant, 3 September 2009.

19 Interview, 1 September 2009.

20 Hong Kong No.42 Director of Audit Report, 31 March 2004. https://www.aud.gov.hk/pdf_e/e42ch04.pdf

21 LegCo Public Accounts Committee Report on Harbour Fest, 2004. http://www.legco.gov.hk/yr03-04/english/pac/reports/42/ch4.pdf

22 Hong Kong Special Administrative Region Court of First Instance 41/2007. http://legalref.judiciary.gov.hk/lrs/common/ju/ju_frame.jsp?DIS=61624&currpage=T

23 LegCo Select Committee to inquire into the handling of the Severe Acute Respiratory Syndrome outbreak by the Government and the Hospital Authority. Minutes of the 22nd Public Hearing, 13 March 2004. https://www.legco.gov.hk/yr03-04/english/sc/sc_sars/reports/tra/040313e.pdf

24 LegCo Select Committee to inquire into the handling of the Severe Acute Respiratory Syndrome outbreak by the Government and the Hospital Authority. Chapter 5, pp. 43–64.

25 Crisis Management: Inter-departmental and Cross Bureau Logistic Support, Expert Committee of SARS, June 2003, http://legco.gov.hk/yr03-04/chinese/sc/sc_sars/reports/tbl/e3b-2.pdf

26 Interview with a former senior civil servant, 30 July 2009; interview with a former senior civil servant, 8 January 2010.

27 Interview with a former senior civil servant, 7 May 2010.

28 Interview, 6 November 2009.

References

Cheung, A. B. L. (2004) 'The Hong Kong System under One Country Being Tested: Article 23, Governance Crisis and the Search for a New Hong Kong Identity.' In Cheng, J. Y. S. (ed.) *The July 1 Protest Rally: Interpreting a Historical Event.* Hong Kong: City University of Hong Kong, pp. 33–69.

Chief Executive's Office (2002) *Code for Principal Officials under the Accountability System.* LC Paper No. CB(2)2462/01-02(01)

Chiu, R. L. H. (2002) Social Equity in Housing: The Hong Kong Special Administrative Region: A Social Sustainability Perspective. *Sustainable Development,* 10, pp. 155–162.

Civil Service Bureau (2003) *Response of the Administration to the Written Submission from the Hong Kong Civil Servants General Union.* September.

Dean, R. (2003) Legislative Developments in Hong Kong: The Hong Kong Jockey Club Fights Back. *Gaming Law Review,* 7(5), pp. 323–328.

East Week (2009) A Loving Heart without Ambition (Chinese). 20 August. https://east-week.my-magazine.me/main/2991

Education Commission (2000) Reform Proposals for the Education System in Hong Kong. September. https://www.e-c.edu.hk/en/publications_and_related_documents/rf1.html.

Finance Bureau (1999) EPP Newsletter. January. https://www.fstb.gov.hk/tb/epp/newsletter/newsletter1/e_newsletter1.pdf.

Fung, A. (2004) Postcolonial Hong Kong Identity: Hybridizing the Local and the National. *Social Identities*, 10(3), pp. 399–414.

Government Press Release (2002a) *Statement by Secretary for Housing, Planning and Lands*. 13 November.

Government Press Release(2002b) *Speech by SJ*. 17 October.

Government Press Release (2002c) *Government Decides to Authorize Soccer Betting*. 26 November.

Government Press Release (2003a) *Chief Executive's Transcript on Basic Law Article 23*. 5 July.

Government Press Release (2003b) *CE Issues Statement*. 16 July.

Government Press Release (2003c) *FS' Statement on His Purchase of a New Car*. 15 March.

Hong Kong Census and Statistics Department (2003) Hong Kong Annual Digest of Statistics. https://www.censtatd.gov.hk/en/data/stat_report/product/B1010003/att/B10100032003AN03B0600.pdf

Hong Kong Census and Statistics Department (2007) Demographic Trends in Hong Kong (1981–2006). https://www.censtatd.gov.hk/en/EIndexbySubject.html?pcode=B1120017&scode=150.

Hong Kong Chief Executive (2003) *Policy Address*. https://www.policyaddress.gov.hk/pa03/eng/policy.htm. Accessed on 25 April 2023.

Hong Kong Court of Appeal (2004) *Judgement: Michael Reid Scott vs. The Government of the Hong Kong Special Administrative Region*.

Hong Kong Economic Journal Monthly (2008) From Joining the Government to Taking Charge of Education Reform (Chinese). 1 February, p. 70.

Hong Kong Economic Times (2002) When Will Lee Lai-kuen and Ho Chi Ping Band Together Again? (Chinese). 22 August. A28.

Hong Kong Financial Secretary (2003) *Budget Speech*. https://www.budget.gov.hk/2003/eng/index.htm.

Hong Kong Government Administrative Wing (2003) *Legislative Council Brief: Internal Review of Remunerations of Senior Executives of Government-funded Bodies*. Ref. CSO/ADMCR2/1136/01

Hong Kong Economic Times (2004) Trade Union Visited Beijing on Wednesday and the Public Servants' Issues Got Attention. 6 November.

Hong Kong Public Opinion Research Institute (2021) Ethnic Identity-Mixed Identity; Hong Konger (Per Poll). 8/1997-12/2021.

Hong Kong Taskforce on Population Policy (2003) *Report*. https://www.info.gov.hk/info/population/eng/pdf/report_eng.pdf

Hood, C. and Lodge, M. (2006) *The Politics of Public Service Bargains. Reward, Competency, Loyalty and Blame*. Oxford: Oxford University Press.

Hospital Authority (2001) *Annual Report*. https://www.ha.org.hk/ho/corpcomm/Annual%20Report/2000-01.pdf

Hospital Authority (2002) *Annual Plan*. https://www.ha.org.hk/ho/corpcomm/Annual%20Plan/2002-03.pdf

Hospital Authority (2008) *Annual Plan*. https://www.ha.org.hk/ho/corpcomm/Annual%20Plan/2008-09.pdf

Hustedt, T. and Salomonsen, H. H. (2014) Ensuring Political Responsiveness: Politicization Mechanisms in Ministerial Bureaucracies. *International Review of Administrative Sciences*, 80(4), pp. 746–765.

Kuan, H-c. and Lau, S-k. (2002) Cognitive Mobilization and Electoral Support for the Democratic Party in Hong Kong. *Electoral Studies*, 21, pp. 561–582.

Lee, F. L. F. (2012) Generational Differences in the Impact of Historical Events: The Tiananmen Square Incident in Contemporary Hong Kong Public Opinion. *International Journal of Public Opinion Research*, 24(2), pp. 141–162.

Legislative Council (2002) *Panel on Housing and Panel on Planning, Lands and Works: Minutes of Joint Meeting*. LC Paper No. CB(1) 577/02-03.

Legislative Council (2003a) *Report of the Bills Committee on Betting Duty (Amendment) Bill*. LC Paper No. CB(2)2657/02-03.

Legislative Council (2003b) *Public Officers Pay Adjustments (2004/2005) Bill*. CSB CR PG/4-085-001/33.

Legislative Council (2003c) *Legal Service Division Report on National Security (Legislative Provisions) Bill*. LC Paper No. LS61/02-03.

Legislative Council (2003d) *Background Brief Prepared by the Legislative Council Secretariat*. LC Paper No. CB(2)1378/02-03(03).

Legislative Council (2003e) *Hansard*. 2 April. https://www.legco.gov.hk/yr02-03/english/counmtg/hansard/cm0402ti-translate-e.pdf

Legislative Council (2004a) *Panel on Education- Minutes of Special Meeting*. LC Paper No. CB(2)1640/03-04.

Legislative Council (2004b) *Minutes of the Meeting*. LC Paper No. CB(3) 163/04-05.

Legislative Council (2004c) *Hansard*. 25 February. https://www.legco.gov.hk/yr03-04/english/counmtg/cm0225ti-translate-e.pdf.

Legislative Council (2005a) *Panel on Public Service: Employment of Non-Civil Service Contract Staff*. LC Paper No. CB(1)1067/05-06(03).

Legislative Council (2005b) *Panel on Public Service: Minutes of Meeting*. LC Paper No. CB(1)901/04-05.

Legislative Council (2005c) *Panel on Health Services: Remuneration of Hospital Authority Staff*. LC Paper No. CB(2)535/04-05(06).

Legislative Council (2006) *Panel on Planning, Lands and Works: Minutes of Meeting* LC Paper No. CB(1)360/06-07(04).

Legislative Council Brief (2001) *Gambling Review-A Consultation Paper*. HAB CR 1/17/93 Pt. 2.

Legislative Council Select Committee (2010) *Report to Inquire into Matters Relating to the Post-Service Work of Mr Leung Chin-man*. Chapter 7.

Li, H.-R. (2012) *An Overview of Hong Kong Basic Law Drafting Process (in Chinese)*. Hong Kong: Joint Publishing Hong Kong.

Li, K. C. (2005) Hong Kong Letter. *RTHK*. 8 January. https://www.edb.gov.hk/tc/about-edb/press/speeches/sed/20050108127521.html.

News.gov.hk (2003) *Regina Ip Resigns*. 16 July.

Oriental Daily (2006) *Drivers Were Angry and Blocked Three Landfills* (in Chinese). 27 January.

Peterson, C. J. (2005) 'Hong Kong's Spring of Discontent: The Rise and Fall of the National Security Bill in 2003.' In Fu, H-l., Petersen, C. J. and Young, S. N. M. (eds.) *National Security and Fundamental Freedoms*. Hong Kong: Hong Kong University Press, pp. 13–62.

SARS Expert Committee (2003) *Summary Report*. https://www.sars-expertcom.gov.hk/english/reports/summary/reports_sumrpt.html.

Scott, I. (2006) The Government and Statutory Bodies in Hong Kong: Centralization and Autonomy. *Public Organization Review,* 6, pp. 185–202.

Security Bureau (2003) *Information on the implementation of Article 23 of the Basic Law*. LC Paper No. CB(2) 1069/02-03(01).

Shaw, R. and Eichbaum, C. (2020) Bubbling up or Cascading down? Public Servants, Political Advisers and Politicization. *Public Administration*, 98, pp. 840–855.

Sing Pao Daily News (2002) *Qian Qichen Urged to Legislate Article 23; the Legal Profession Worried That Legislation Subversion Would Threaten Freedom of Expression (in Chinese)*. 26 June, A14.

Siu, A. and Wong, R. Y. C. (2004) Economic Impact of SARS: The Case of Hong Kong. *Asian Economic Papers*, 3(1), pp. 62–83.

South China Morning Post (2004) *The Full Text of Dr Yeoh's Resignation Letter*. 8 July.

South China Morning Post (2007) *Civil Servants Can Be Too Inflexible, Says Sarah Liao*. July.

Transport Bureau (2001) *Legislative Council Brief: Electronic Road Pricing*. 24 April. TBCR 2/1/2061/89 Pt 16

Waterman, W. R. and Meier, K. J. (1998) Principal-Agent Models: An Expansion? *Journal of Public Administration Research and Theory*, 8(2), pp. 173–202.

Wong, S. H.-W. (2015) *Electoral Politics in Post-1997 Hong Kong: Protest, Patronage, and the Media*. Singapore: Springer Singapore Pte. Limited.

Xinhua (2005) Court of Final Appeal: Pay Cuts for Civil Servants Lawful. 13 July. http://www.chinadaily.com.cn/english/doc/2005-07/13/content_459901.htm

Yung, C. (2006) Truckers Lift Rubbish Blockade. *The Standard*. 28 January. p. A10.

4 Reform impact and Political Appointment System

2005–2012

4.1 Social-economic-political contexts during 2005–2012

With the economic recovery and reduced supply of government-subsidised housing, the problems of housing-related poverty and deprivation deteriorated during the period (Wong and Chan, 2019). The private housing price index rose from 92.7 in 2006 to 206.2 (Rating and Valuation Department, 2022). About half of Hong Kong population could not afford private housing and lived in government-subsidised housing units then. However, the supply of the public rental housing (PRH) and subsidised home ownership housing, two major housing welfare programmes in Hong Kong, declined during the period. The average production of PRH declined from 16,970 during 2002–2008 to 13,416 during 2009–2011. At the same time, the number of applicants for PRH flats more than doubled from 110,000 in the mid-2000s to 222,200 at the end of 2012. During 2003–2011, the supply of subsidised flats for sale almost ceased, with the average annual production stood at negligible 716 during the period of 2002–2011 (Legislative Council Secretariat, 2013).

Central People's Government (CPG)'s proactive policy to integrate Hong Kong's economic development into the development of Pearl River Delta areas had brought Hong Kong wealth but also intensified conflicts over infrastructure siting and use of local public services. The young protesters' concerns towards high expenditure, environmental pollution and social injustice of Express Rail Way linking Hong Kong and Guangzhou, whose budget was passed by the Legislative Council (LegCo) in 2008, were not addressed effectively by the Hong Kong government (Sung, 2019). After the introduction of the Mainland and Hong Kong Closer Economic Partnership Arrangement in June 2003, there were conflicts due to increasing tourists from mainland China and parallel goods traders, whose purchase of daily necessities and luxurious goods had pushed up the living costs of Hong Kong people. The increasing number of babies born in Hong Kong by parents living in mainland China also caused anxieties that essential goods and services like baby formula, education and housing would be in shortage. The number of protests about these issues reported by local newspapers increased from 1

DOI: 10.4324/9781003195924-4

in 2011 to 9 in 2014 and 2015, respectively. These protests were part of the localist movement in Hong Kong which later turned radicalised and militant (Yuen and Chung, 2018). According to a survey by a local university, during 2008–2012, the percentage of respondents identifying themselves as Hong Kongese increased from 16.7% to 23.3%, while that of respondents identifying themselves as Chinese but also Hong Kongese declined from 24.9% to 22% during the period (Chinese University of Hong Kong, 2020).

Some localists turned to be radicalised, preferring to adopt a violent approach in protests and criticised the traditional nationalist democratic movement led by pan-democratic political parties such as the Democratic Party, Civic Party and Confederation of Trade Union (Yuen and Chung, 2018). The 'post-80s' young protesters were disappointed at the hierarchical and exclusive practices within pro-democracy political parties and chose to organise social movements (such as the anti-Express Rail Link movement) without following the instructions of the latter. Some of these protesters desired for immediate adoption of 'one person one vote' to directly elect CE and all LegCo members (Lam-Knott, 2018).

Hong Kong Basic Law commits to gradually reforming the methods of selecting the Chief Executive (CE)[1] and electing LegCo members, and returning these political actors by universal suffrage.[2] Tsang Yam-kuen's administration in 2007–2012 placed the political reform as one of its top priorities. The CE election in 2007 was more competitive due to the nomination of a Civic Party candidate Alan Leong Kah-kit from the pro-democracy camp. Tsang Yam-kuen's election campaign platform pledged to reform the political system towards the goal of implementing the 'dual universal suffrage' (shuang puxuan), and encouraged more participation of civil society in policymaking (Fenghuang Net, 2007). In 2010, Tsang, in his role as CE, successfully got LegCo to approve the election reform proposal, expanding the number of seats for geographical and functional constituencies from 30 to 35, respectively, including five district council seats directly elected by voters (Cheng, 2021).

However, the 2010 electoral reform proposal fell short of the expectations of some political parties in the pro-democracy camp, including Civic Party and League of Social Democrats, who orchestrated the LegCo resignation and by-elections in five geographical constituencies in the hope of mobilising citizens' support to their demand for abolishing functional constituencies by 2012 and implementing the election of CE through universal suffrage without pre-election candidate filtering by 2017 (Civic Party, 2009; BBC news, 2010). While the voter turn-out rate was as low as 17%, the by-elections reflected the internal conflicts of the pro-democracy camp, and polarised opinions among Hong Kong citizens towards the pace and direction of political reforms (Cheng, 2011).

Tsang administration encountered difficulties to obtain public and legislators' support for its policy initiatives. A survey showed that local citizens' satisfaction rate towards Hong Kong government dropped quickly from 42.5% at March 2008 to 19.9% in June 2012.[3] While the pro-democratic camp continued to have only around 35% of the total seats in 2004–2008 and 2008–2012 LegCo sessions, they controlled a critical minority in the geographical constituency, which enabled them to veto the bills proposed by the administration (Branigan, 2008). The number of bills proposed, tabled and passed in LegCo dropped by about 48.5%, 51% and 46.5% during Tsang administration compared with Tung administration (Fong, 2014).

4.2 Political-administrative relations under Tsang Yam-kuen administration (2005–2007)

Mr Tsang Yam-kuen, the then Chief Secretary for Administration (CSA), won the by-election and succeeded Tung Chee-hwa as CE for the remaining term of Tung administration. Tsang's administration kept all the 'outsider' political appointees during Tung administration except appointing a new legal professional to succeed Ms Elsie Leung Oi-sie to be the Secretary for Justice.[4] But Tsang appeared to trust civil servants more. Instead of promoting the then Financial Secretary (FS) Henry Tang Ying-yen, coming from an industrial tycoon family, Tsang appointed Rafael Hui Si-yan, a retired senior civil servant with experiences in economic and financial policies to be the CSA.

The 2005 by-election manifesto showed Tsang's governing philosophy. He believed in the principle of 'small government and big market' and the 'market-led and government facilitating' economic development mode. Some business and banking industry tycoons such as Henry Fok Ying-tung and David Li Kwok-po joined his election campaign team, showing their support for Tsang's low-tax and liberal policies (Leung and Cheung, 2005). As a career Administrative Officer (AO), Tsang was also supported by civil servants, particularly those in the AO grade (Cheung, 2005). He also enjoyed high public support (over 70 out of 100 marks) during the election campaign period according to the opinion polls (Chung, 2005). He proposed to move forward the political reform, to realise the 'dual universal suffrage' goals set by the Basic Law. He also promised to involve civil society and listen to public opinion in policymaking (China News Service, 2007).

Tsang strengthened the CE office's staff capacity to communicate with the media, political parties and LegCo members. He created a senior civil servant post, Permanent Secretary (PS) for CE's Office, who would oversee the coordination among bureaux and departments to ensure effective implementation of CE's policies and directives, as well as the Executive Council (ExCo)'s Secretariat. The PS for CE's Office would share much of the work from the political appointed Director of the CE's Office, who then could devote time to political and policy work, such as securing support by political stakeholders for government work, conducting research on government major policies, and

Enclosure 1 to EC(2005-06)6

Existing Organisation Chart of the Chief Executive's Office

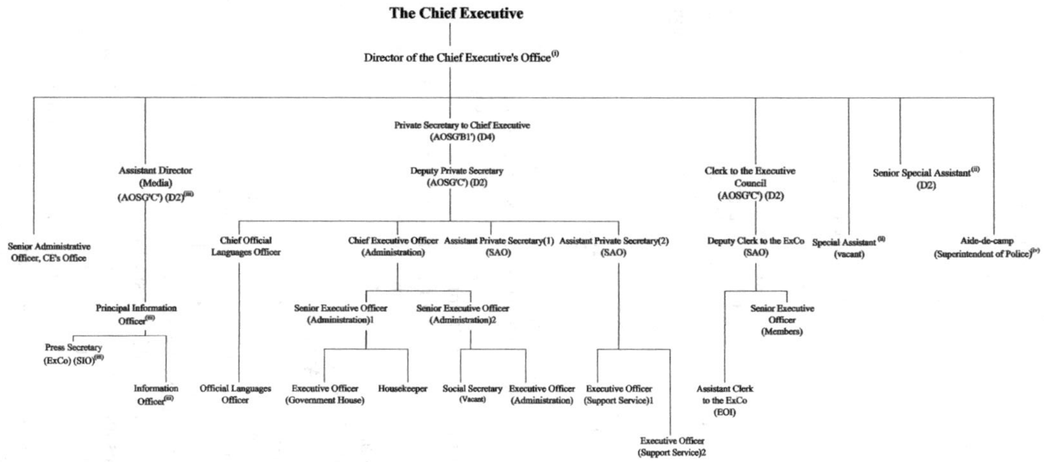

Legend:

(i) DCEO is an non-civil service appointment and vacant since 7.1.2005. A supernumerary AOSG'A'1(D8) post, designated as Permanent Secretary, CE's Office is created for the period 1.8.2005 to 31.1.2006
(ii) Non-civil service appointment
(iii) On establishment of Information Services Department
(iv) On loan from Hong Kong Police Force
AOSG - Administrative Officer Staff Grade
SAO - Senior Administrative Officer

Figure 4.1 Organisation chart of the Chief Executive's Office: 2005.

Source: Legislative Council Finance Committee Establishment Subcommittee, 7 December 2005, EC (2005-06)6. https://www.legco.gov.hk/yr05-06/english/fc/esc/papers/e05-06e.pdf

setting policy objectives and priorities. Tsang also created a new permanent non-civil service post, to assist the implementation of public relation (PR) strategies and coordination of the PR-related work (Figure 4.1).

Tsang re-titled the Principal Official Accountability System (POAS) to Political Appointment System (PAS), expanded the number of non-official members of the ExCo from 7 to 15 and pledged to involve them at an earlier stage of policymaking processes. According to a former ExCo non-official member, the ExCo under Tsang administration took into view points of its non-official members seriously and even rejected some policy papers proposed by the Principal Officials (POs) of the bureaus, which did not happen during Tung's second administration.[5]

In general, the political-administrative relations during this period were characteristic of being 'collaborative' and 'mutually respectful'. Tsang and the PO team continued to carry out the policies set on the agenda during Tung administration. Tsang's policy style was less hands-on than Tung. The policy committee chaired by the Chief Secretary was normally not attended by Tsang. Some POs, unlike those under Tung administration, had more autonomy to manage their portfolios.[6] Tsang was said to be able to control civil servant subordinates more easily than Tung did, because of his career background:

> When Mr. Tung wanted to do something, very often he was told by the senior civil servant: 'No sir, we can't do that.' No civil servant would dare to talk to Donald [Tsang Yam-kuen] in that way. 'Don't tell me it's impossible, I know it.'[7]

4.2.1   Case 4.1: Proposing electoral reforms

A major agenda during this period was to reform the CE and LegCo members' election methods (constitutional development). The reform was put on the agenda by Tung Chee Hwa in early 2004, in response to the community's concerns about the constitutional development. Tung set up a Constitutional Development Task Force in January 2004, headed by the CSA and including the Secretary for Justice and the Secretary for Constitutional Affairs (SCA) as the members, to consult the public, CPG and other stakeholders about the related legislative processes.

After Tsang was elected the CE in July 2005, the Task Force proposed an electoral package that enhanced the level of participation of district council members, most of whom were directly elected, in the CE's Election Committee and LegCo. However, the pro-democracy camp in the LegCo demanded universal suffrage of CE and LegCo members in 2007 and 2008, respectively, which had already been ruled out by the National People's Congress Standing Committee (Legislative Council Secretariat, 2009). The then CS and SCA involved in formulating the package were both career AOs. They helped promote the reform bill and defended criticism from the pro-democracy camp and the US government (Government Press Release, 2005, 2007).

In Case 4.1, the CE and two political appointees (CSA and SCA) were all former AOs. They shared the same AO grade culture and similar career paths. Their civil servant subordinates involved in the policymaking, including PS for the CE's Office and PS for Constitutional Affairs, were also career AOs. The political-administrative working relationship in this case was collaborative. The roles of CE and the two political appointees are similar to those in Image IV, where the former senior civil servants' political roles were strengthened in the new political positions.

Based on Case 4.1, H2, H3a and H4a are confirmed. The following hypothesis is proposed:

> Under the structural role differentiation between political appointees and civil servants, the political-administrative relations in policymaking are likely to be collaborative when: 1) the policy formulation is partly controlled by the hierarchically higher level jurisdiction; 2) the political appointees and civil servants have similar career backgrounds; and 3) the issue involves intensive public mood.

4.2.2   Case 4.2: Legislating mandatory nutrition labelling

The government proposed to impose a mandatory nutrition labelling scheme on prepackaged food products in March 2003, in order to protect public health and ensure food safety. Some LegCo members, medical professionals and patients' groups supported the proposal, while other LegCo members and some food trade representatives were concerned with the increased costs and wished to reduce the scope of proposal (LegCo, 2005). Although the government conducted public consultation on the proposal as early as in November 2003, the Food and Health (FH) Bureau only tabled the amendment bill in April 2008. Business interest groups and a Liberal Party LegCo member publicly expressed concerns over the exempt conditions for low-sales-volume products, on the ground that the proposed regulation would limit consumer choice (Leung, 2008). The Hong Kong General Chamber of Commerce also publicly advocated that the proposed bill should reduce the number of core nutrients in the label from 7 to 3 (Hong Kong General Chamber of Commerce, 2008). Under the political pressure, the FH Bureau proposed an amendment that relaxed the exemption conditions for low-sales-volume products, but were voted down due to opposition by the pro-democracy camp (South China Morning Post, 2008). Nevertheless, the bureau did not change the original number of nutrients to be claimed in the label, which was not consistent with CE's Tsang Yam-kuen's liberal policy orientation. A major reason was that Tsang respected the preferences of the then Secretary for FH, a medical professional, to prioritise the protection of public health in designing the regulation.[8]

The political-administrative relations in Case 4.2 are characteristic of mutual respect. Secretary for FH Bureau's medical professional background explained his preferences for a stringent nutrition labelling legislation advocated by the medical professional association. While there is no direct evidence showing that the bureau civil servants opposed the stringent legislation, the vocal opposition from the business sector could not have been ignored by the senior civil servants involved in policymaking, and the civil-servant-turned CE. The bureau finally compromised in formulating the bill, addressing some concerns of the business sector. With civil-servant-turned CE's support for the bill, bureau civil servants respected the outsider PO's preferences.

Based on Case 4.2, H2, H3d and part of H4d are confirmed, but not H1 nor H4a. The following hypothesis is proposed:

> Under the structural role differentiation between political appointees and civil servants, the political-administrative relations in policymaking are likely to be mutually respectful when: 1) the issue involves intensive public mood; 2) the bureau political appointee has technical capability on the issue and would like to control policymaking; 3) there are different professional and career backgrounds between the bureau political appointee and civil servants; 4) the hierarchically higher level jurisdiction respects the bureau political appointee's policymaking autonomy.

4.3   Political-administrative relations under Tsang Yam-kuen administration (2007–2012)

Among 15 POs appointed by Tsang in his second term, nine were career civil servants, including eight career AOs and one career Immigration Officer (Table 4.1). Since all POs were members of ExCo, AOs' values and policy styles could dominate policymaking due to their majority numbers.

Comparing to his first term, Tsang was more able to govern according to his own philosophy and agenda because the PO team was formed by himself. For instance, one PO and a bureau civil servant were said to have different policy preferences with Tsang in his first term as CE (2005–2007):

> I know Donald [Tsang Yam-kuen] never thinks the policy **A** is going down the right way. He is deadly against the reform in the first place. … He told me the point blank about this. And he brought in the **B** programme. That is against the advice of the bureau at the time. **C** [the PO of the bureau] banged the table in ExCo over the B programme.[9]

To strengthen support for the POs in dealing with governance and political work, and to reduce political work of civil servants and maintain their political neutrality, Tsang introduced Under Secretaries (USs) and Political Assistants (PAs) under the PAS (Table 4.2). USs were responsible for full range of

Table 4.1 Principal Officials (policy secretaries) of HKSARG[a] in July 2007

Position titles	Career background	Political party affiliation before taking the position
• Chief Secretary for Administration	• An industrialist	• Liberal Party
• Financial Secretary	• A career AO in HKSARG	• Nil
• Secretary for Justice	• A private legal professional	• Nil
• Secretary for Education	• A career AO in HKSARG	• Nil
• Secretary for Commerce and Economic Development	• A private sector financial manager	• Nil
• Secretary for Constitutional and Mainland Affairs	• A career AO in HKSARG	• Nil
• Secretary for Security	• A career Immigration Officer in HKSARG	• Nil
• Secretary for Food and Health	• A career public hospital manager	• Nil
• Secretary for the Civil Service	• A career AO in HKSARG	• Nil
• Secretary for Home Affairs	• A media professional	• Democratic Alliance for the Betterment and Progress of Hong Kong
• Secretary for Labour and Welfare	• A career AO in HKSARG	• Nil
• Secretary for Financial Services and the Treasury	• A university professor	• Nil
• Secretary for Development	• A career AO in HKSARG	• Nil
• Secretary for the Environment	• A career AO in HKSARG	• Nil
• Secretary for Transport and Housing	• A career AO in HKSARG	• Nil

Source: Government Press Release, 'New team of Principal Officials appointed', 23 June 2007.

[a]Hong Kong Special Administrative Region Government.

political work, particularly the LegCo business, and assisted POs with setting policy objectives and formulating policy initiatives and political strategies to achieve the objectives. PAs would take political liaison work with the media and the public, and provide political advice in policy formulation, lobbying and communication. Under the PAS, civil servants would continue to support POs' work in implementing, formulating, explaining and defending government policies; with reduced political workload, civil servants were expected to have more time to conduct policy analysis (Constitutional and Mainland Affairs Bureau, 2007).

Table 4.2 Background of Under Secretaries and Political Assistants under Tsang Yam-kuen Administration[a]

Position titles	Career background	Political party affiliation before taking the position
• Under Secretary for Commerce and Economic Development	• A legal professional and a former district councilor (government appointed)	• Democratic Alliance for the Betterment and Progress of Hong Kong
• Under Secretary for Constitutional and Mainland Affairs (2008–2009)	• A career AO in HKSARG	• Nil
• Under Secretary for Constitutional and Mainland Affairs (2009–2012)	• A career AO in HKSARG	• Nil
• Under Secretary for Financial Services and the Treasury	• A journalist and public relation manager	• Nil
• Under Secretary for Education	• A business manager	• Nil
• Under Secretary for the Environment	• A university professional	• Nil
• Under Secretary for Food and Health	• A university professional	• Nil
• Under Secretary for Transport and Housing	• A newspaper reporter and writer	• Nil
• Under Secretary for Security	• A career Immigration Officer	• Nil
• Under Secretary for Home Affairs	• A business manager	
• Political Assistant to the Financial Secretary	• A newspaper editor and writer	• Nil
• Political Assistant to the Secretary for Development	• A legal professional and a former district councilor	• Hong Kong Association for Democracy and People's Livelihood; Democratic Alliance for the Betterment and Progress of Hong Kong
• Political Assistant to the Secretary for Education	• A business manager	• Liberal Party
• Political Assistant to the Secretary for the Environment	• A former AO, a newspaper editor and business manager	• Nil
• Political Assistant to the Secretary for Financial Services and the Treasury	• A legal professional	• Nil

(*continued*)

Table 4.2 (Continued)

Position titles	Career background	Political party affiliation before taking the position
• Political Assistant to the Secretary for Food and Health	• A university researcher and a TV commentator	• Nil
• Political Assistant to the Secretary for Home Affairs	• A financial service manager	• Democratic Alliance for the Betterment and Progress of Hong Kong
• Political Assistant to the Secretary for Labour and Welfare	• A think tank manager and TV news reporter	• Nil
• Political Assistant to the Secretary for Security	• A career police officer	• Nil

Sources: Government Press Release, 'CE appoints Under Secretaries', 20 May 2008; 'CE appoints Political Assistants', 22 May 2008; 'CE appoints two Under Secretaries', 22 October 2009.

[a]Appointed in May 2008 and October 2009.

4.3.1   *Explaining collaborative political-administrative relations*

4.3.1.1   *Case 4.3: Regional Education Hub*

The idea to make Hong Kong a Regional Education Hub (REH) was publicly proposed by the Secretary for Education and Manpower (SEM) Professor Li Kwok-cheung, a former university vice-chancellor as early as in 2005. The objective was to attract fee-paying non-local students to study in Hong Kong. The proposal needed policy support from other bureaus such as relaxing admission quota for non-local students of public-funded institutions, less stringent immigration control for non-local students' part-time work and land for non-local students' boarding facilities.[10]

While the Tsang administration announced the establishment of a Steering Committee chaired by the CSA in 2006–2007 to study the issue, it was not until Tsang was reelected as CE in 2007 that the measures to deliver the REH were announced in the Policy Address. These measures include making available sites for the development of international schools and hostel facilities, increasing the admission quotas for non-local students to local tertiary institutions, relaxing employment restrictions on non-local students and providing scholarships to non-local students, similar to the proposal put forward earlier by Professor Li.[11]

A former senior official involved in the process suggested that Tsang did not intend to keep Professor Li in the government, and therefore delayed the announcement of the REH policy until he was reelected. [12]

After Tsang was reelected in 2007, he appointed a new SEM to replace Professor Li. The working relations between the CE, CSA, SEM and PS for Education and Manpower were collaborative in delivering the REH. All of them were career AOs. The policy mainly relaxed regulatory measures, which benefited the education sector without increasing large amount of recurrent public expenditure. Following the 2007 Policy Address, Tsang announced more supportive measures for the REH in 2009–2010 Policy Address, such as allowing Mainland students to pursue studies in non-local programmes at degree level or above in Hong Kong. The public mood is supportive of the government.

Based on Case 4.3, H1a, H2 and H3a are confirmed, but not any sub-hypothesis of H4 is relevant. The following hypothesis is proposed:

Under the structural role differentiation between political appointees and civil servants, the political-administrative relations in policymaking are likely to be collaborative when: 1) political appointees and civil servants have similar career backgrounds; 2) the policy is distributive and of low costs for the government.

4.3.2   Case 4.4: Adopting Statutory Minimum Wage

It was surprising that Tsang administration, upholding the governing principle of 'small government and big market', adopted the statutory minimum wage in 2011. Three contextual factors were associated with the legislation: (1) over a decade of public debates, policy practices and business-labour negotiation have facilitated the consensus building among political-administrative-economic elites and other members of the public; (2) Tsang's recognition of the need to reconcile heightened societal and political conflicts associated with a widening wealth gap; (3) the good economic condition.

Setting a statutory minimum wage had been on Hong Kong LegCo's agenda since 1998. Despite initial business opposition due to economic recession and high unemployment, more legislators came to support the idea (Lee, 2010). The government adopted an incremental approach to demonstrate to the opponents that legislating minimum wage was the most effective to tackle the problems of low wages.

Under the Tung administration, the government required all its contractors to pay employees the average wage as published by the Census and Statistics Department in 2004; then in early 2005, the issue was on the agenda of a tripartite (labour, business and government) consultative body for negotiation. Under the Tsang administration in 2006, the government further the agenda by initiating the voluntary wage protection movement (WPM) where employers were encouraged to provide wages to cleaners and security guards at an average market level. After Tsang was reelected as CE in 2007, and with a midterm review of WPM showing that less than 10% of employers had joined, the government started the legislation work.

Tsang nominated Mr Matthew Cheung Kin-chung, a retired AO who was involved in labour policy formulation, to be appointed as the Secretary for Labour and Welfare, being in charge of the Minimum Wage Legislation. Mr Cheung used to be the Commissioner for Labour during 1999–2000, and PS for Labour during 2002–2007.[13] He was not only experienced in handling minimum wage issues, but also supportive of adopting a statutory minimum wage. The WPM was said to be an idea from Mr Cheung when he was the PS for Labour.[14] While the Secretary for Economic Development and Labour then Mr Stephen Ip, also a career AO, was committed to promoting harmonious labour relations for social stability and economic prosperity.[15] According to the survey conducted during 2009–2012, a majority (20 out of 30, 67%) of senior civil servants supported Minimum Wage Legislation, close to that of a mass opinion poll (70% being supportive) conducted in 2010 (Burns and Li, 2015).

In Case 4.4, the working relations between the CE, the AO-turned POs and senior civil servants were collaborative in setting the Minimum Wage Legislation on the agenda and had it passed by the LegCo eventually. The similar career background and shared policy goals of the political and administrative officials facilitated their collaboration despite the business sector's opposition and divisive political environment.

The case confirmed H1a, H2, H3a and H4a, and the following hypothesis is proposed:

> Under the structural role differentiation between political appointees and civil servants, the political-administrative relations in policymaking are likely to be collaborative: 1) when political appointees and civil servants have similar career backgrounds; 2) when the public mood is intensive; 3) there is consensus between the political-administrative-economic elites and other members of the public.

4.3.3   *Explaining adversarial political-administrative relations*

4.3.3.1   *Working relations between POs and senior civil servants*

While the overall working relations between POs and their civil servant subordinates are collaborative under Tsang administration because more POs are appointed from civil service, there are cases of disagreement between political appointed PO and his/her civil servant subordinate even though they both have AO backgrounds. One AO-turned PO explained how his/her working relation with a PS did not work out:

> I look for people who have passion, the passion to make things better. I look for people who are committed to the job. I look for people who don't shy away from difficulties, who prepare to argue.

This PO, despite being a career AO, had a sense of urgency and was willing to take the political risks as a political appointed official in proposing innovative policies.

First,

> I wouldn't probably be advocating the same... have I not been a PO... I was quite prepared to say sorry publicly if I got wrong this time. With that, perhaps my senior, my counterparts felt that since there was a body with this strong commitment to be held responsible, they would allow me to do it.

Second,

> This element of timing, for the first time, comes into my mind. Very consciously, you have a term. You want to do things you do it now.[16]

4.3.3.2   Case 4.5: Revitalising Industrial Building Scheme

Like many industrialised cities, Hong Kong experienced economic structural changes. Many factories in Hong Kong have moved to places of low cost, and there has been increasing demand for residential and commercial service buildings in the city centres. To utilise the industrial buildings that were left vacant or otherwise illegally used for other purposes, the CE Tsang Yam-kuen announced in 2009–2010 Policy Address four regulatory measures to encourage owners to redevelop or converse the industrial buildings. This was an initiative from the Development Bureau led by its Secretary Ms Carrie Lam Cheng Yuet-ngor (Lam). Due to the rising housing prices and the LegCo investigation of the connection between a senior civil servant's post-retirement work in real estate organisations and his role in formulating housing and land policies in the government,[17] some civil servants were said to be reluctant to handle development projects that collaborate with the private sector. Lam was aware of such concerns and pledged that the bureau would be transparent and open to public monitoring in handling such projects, while would not shy away from implementing projects benefiting the public interest.[18]

Lam had a reputation of being a risk-taking and strong-minded official.[19] According to an interviewee, she preferred working with proactive civil servants who would argue with her and get things done despite the difficulties. In formulating the revitalising industrial building scheme, she overruled civil servants' suggestions of using an incremental approach, such as offering fee discount to the owners to observe the uncertain market reaction, and instead waived fee for change of land use.[20]

In this case, the working relations between the PO and the senior civil servants were somewhat conflictual because of their different structural role and attitudes towards political risks.

The case confirmed H1a and H4a, but not H3a. The following hypothesis is proposed:

> Under the structural role differentiation between political appointees and civil servants, the political-administrative relations in policymaking are likely to be adversarial when 1) political appointees and civil servants have similar career backgrounds; 2) when the issue involves intensive public mood; 3) when the risk of invoking public criticism is perceived high by civil servants.

Even before the introduction of the POAS, there was structural friction between generalist AOs in the bureau and professional grade civil servants in the department. The former attended more to cross-departmental issues such as fiscal sustainability and political acceptance. The latter attended more to the technical and procedural issues within the specific policy or regulatory domain. As discussed in Chapter 2 and shown by the case of Education Reform in 2000, the introduction of the POAS was in part an effort to strengthen political control over departmental civil servants of professional grades. Under the PAS and with a contentious political environment, we observed open conflicts between a departmental civil servant, a bureau civil servant and political appointees.

4.3.4   Case 4.6: Internet Learning Support Programme

To mitigate the impact of digital divide on learning, in 2009–2010 Policy Address, CE announced that students in need shall be provided convenient and suitable internet learning opportunities through collaboration between the community, the business sector and the government. The FS Mr John Tsang Chun-wah allocated HKD 500 million for the initiative. Internet Learning Support Programme (ILSP) is a five-year programme that enables low-income students to have affordable computers and internet access for online learning, and provide them technical and training support. The Office of the Government Chief Information Officer (OGCIO) launched an open tendering to select one implementer of the programme during May–July 2010.[21] The government later on announced that the proposals of two organisations, eInclusion Foundation Limited (eInclusion) and Hong Kong Council of Social Services (HKCSS), were both of merit, and the two organisations would implement the programme in two geographical zones, respectively (the dual-implementer approach).[22]

The Chief Information Officer Mr Jeremy Godfrey, a contract-term civil servant, disagreed with this decision nor with the government narratives about the tendering process. He resigned from his post before the launch of the programme and submitted a note to the LegCo, explaining that he objected to the dual-implementer approach because it was not cost-effective to serve the best interest of low-income families; as the Controlling Officer of the programme budget, he felt unable to defend the decision. He also revealed that FS indicated to him that iProA[23] had important skills relevant to the programme before the tendering process. When the proposals were being evaluated, OGCIO received a phone call from the FS office that reminded Mr Godfrey the desired outcome preferred by the FS. When it turned out, the HKCSS received the highest score by the evaluation panel, the Permanent Secretary for Communications and Technology (PSCT) was quoted by Mr Godfrey that it was a political assignment to award the programme to the iProA, which came from beyond FS. Mr Godfrey preferred that the two organisations could collaborate to implement the programme across the region so that the service target could benefit from the strength of the two organisations. However, the collaboration discussion failed, and the PSCT overruled Godfrey's objection and adopted a dual-implementer approach to launch the ILSP.[24]

In this case, apparently the conflicts were between the civil servants in the bureau and the department. The source of conflicts was in fact the difference between political appointees' preference and the preference of civil servants in professional grade with regard to the selection of programme implementers. The tendering process received LegCo members' attention and criticism that the government was suspect to favour iProA because of its connection to a pro-establishment political party. The political appointees in this case were motivated by accountability to their political constituents. The department civil servant was motivated by multiple accountability relations, including being bureaucratically accountable to their superiors, professionally accountable to their fellows and the public, and legally accountable (when managing public funds) to the LegCo. In this case, the civil servant was appointed on a contract-term from outside the government, and therefore his norm of upholding bureaucratic accountability was relatively weak. Instead, he felt strong obligations to uphold legal accountability in his role as the Controlling Officer. He tendered the resignation and spoke out to defend his decision in order to uphold the legal and professional accountability. Mr Godfrey explained the reason of his open submission to the IT and Broadcast Panel of the LegCo about his resignation:

> Regrettably, the Government has made use of my name in its misleading narrative of events. If I do not speak up, I could be considered to bear some responsibility for allowing the Panel to be misled, to the detriment of my self-respect and my reputation.[25]

The case confirmed H1a, H2, H3b, but not H4a. The following hypothesis is proposed:

> Under the structural role differentiation between political appointees and civil servants, the political-administrative relations in policymaking are likely to be adversarial: 1) when political appointees and civil servants have different career and professional backgrounds; 2) political appointees lack technical capability of handling the issue; and 3) the public mood is intensive.

*4.3.4.1 Working relations between Under Secretaries, Political
Assistants and civil servants*

The roles of USs and PAs overlap in part with those of civil servants, such as attending LegCo meetings, lobbying political stakeholders and managing media relations, but they are motivated by different perspectives and purposes. This sometimes leads to tension between the two parties in their policy and political work.

Some USs drafted policy papers in person, which used to be undertaken by civil servants in the bureau. These USs, particularly those professionals, perceived that the generalist AOs in the bureau lacked subject knowledge to make the right assessment in the policy development, nor did they have the political acumen or courage to manage and decide on issues that were objected by certain societal groups.[26]

PAs' liaison role overlaps with that of the press secretary. In one bureau, the press secretary wrote and published press releases, and managed their relationship with the media in a politically neutral way, while the PA would *'talk to one paper, but not the other, feeding them with positive message so that it can pave the way for the policy'*.[27] In another bureau, the PA took over the speech-drafting task from the press secretary, who was only required to give some input.[28]

PAs also oversaw the delivery of some projects that involve the business sector, which civil servants would prefer not to get involved in fear of being seen as colluding with the latter.[29] PAs brought political contacts from outside the government, and political perspectives to the government internal policy deliberation.[30]

Both USs and PAs undertook some of the political lobbying work previously done by civil servants, in order to assist the POs' policy work. They handled requests from LegCo members, received lobbyists of interest groups, consulted stakeholders on policy proposals, attended district council meetings, chatted with journalists about policy backgrounds and set up government advisory bodies to formulate new policies.[31]

4.4 Evaluating the PAS under Tsang administration

As the title change from 'POAS' to 'PAS' suggested, the political accountability in the form of PO resignation was downplayed by Tsang administration. Although the capability, personal conduct and performance of POs, USs and PAs continued to be questioned by some public members (Table 4.3), none of these political appointees stepped down to shoulder political accountability. The LegCo questions and public concerns about the operation of the POAS

Table 4.3 Public concerns about the operation of the POAS and institutional development of the PAS

Public concerns	Institutional development of the PAS
• Year 2007: Concerns about the appointment procedures and selection criteria of USs and PAs.[a]	• Year 2008: Establish the Appointment Committee chaired by the CE, and interviewing panels involving relevant Secretaries of Departments and Director(s) of Bureaus. The relevant POs will be consulted and agree before the exact posting of USs and PAs is decided.[b] Year 2012: 1 The posts of Under Secretaries and Political Assistants were open to public application through the appeal of the CE-elect. 2 The government announced the selection criteria of US(s),[c] stages of selection, the number of applicants for the posts of USs, as well as the membership and the meetings of the Selection Committee chaired by the CE-elect.[d]
• Year 2007: Remuneration of POs is much higher than POs of overseas countries and higher than LegCo members.[e]	• Year 2008: *Independent Commission on Remuneration for Members of the Executive Council and the Legislature* was renamed as *Independent Commission on Remuneration for Members of the Executive Council and the Legislature, and Officials under the Political Appointment System* (the Independent Commission), to advise the government on matters related to the remuneration for officials under the Political Appointment System.[f]
• Years between 2002 and 2007: Concerns about declaration of interests by POs under the POAS.[g]	• Year 2011–2012: revised Code for Officials Under PAS (with effect from July 2012), to expand relevant rules such as: 1 Requiring politically appointed officials (PAOs) to place the investments or interests that may be in conflict of interests with their official duties in a 'blind trust' (5.8); 2 Clarifying that provisions about soliciting and accepting advantages by public servants under the Prevention of Bribery Ordinance and the Independent Commission Against Corruption Ordinance apply to the PAOs under PAS (5.9); 3 Requiring the PAOs to consider whether acceptance of advantage would (b) place the PAO in a position of obligation to the offerer or under any improper obligation; compromise the judgement of the PAO or to lead to a reasonable perception of such compromise (5.13); 4 Clarifying the sanctions in the event of allegation of breach of the relevant provision (7.9).

(*continued*)

Table 4.3 (Continued)

Public concerns	Institutional development of the PAS
• Year 2008: Concerns about the remuneration of US(s) and PA(s).[h]	• Year 2012: Remuneration of political appointees is reviewed by the Independent Commission, recommending lowering the cash remuneration for Political Assistants to 30% of that for Directors of Bureaus[i]

[a]Hong Kong Constitutional and Mainland Affairs Bureau. Report on Further Development of Political Appointment System. October 2007.

[b]Government Press Release. Government Response to Comments on Expansion of Political Appointment System and Constitutional Development. 22 June 2008.

[c]The CE-elect emphasised that the appointment of politically appointed officials, including US(s) and PAs should be based on merit, including vision, commitment, ability and political capability. LC Paper No. CB(2)2164/11-12(01). May 2012.

[d]Government Press Release. 39 Under Secretary candidates enter next stage of selection process. 11 June 2012.

[e]Government Press Release. LCQ13: Remuneration Package for Officials under Political Appointment System. 12 December 2007.

[f]Government Press Release. Independent Commission on Remuneration for Members of Exco and Legco, and Officials under the Political Appointment System. 17 March 2008.

[g]Background brief prepared by Legislative Council Secretariat: System of declaration of interests by the Chief Executive and Principal Officials under the Accountability System. 16 November 2009. LC Paper No. CB(2)244/09-10(04).

[h]Legislative Council Ref: CB2/PL/CA LC Paper No. CB(2)2806/07-08. Panel on Constitutional Affairs, Minutes of meeting. 16 June 2008.

[i]Report on the Remuneration Package for Politically-Appointed Officials serving in the Fourth-Term HKSAR Government.

and PAS shaped further institutionalisation of the PAS in respect of appointment, remuneration, political activities and conduct of political appointees.

The political-administrative relations under Tsang administration were generally collaborative, compared to those under Tung administration. Some civil servant interviewees opined that this was because civil-servant-turned POs knew how the government system worked and were more able to get things done than outsider POs.[32]

The economy under the Tsang administration also recovered, and the need to reduce the size of civil service was no longer urgent. After year 2007–2008, the general civil service open recruitment freeze was lifted. As at 1 April 2010, the Civil Service establishment and strength were 162,832 and 156,573, respectively, representing an increase of 2.2% for establishment and an increase of 1.8% for strength since end-March 2007.[33] The number of years required for a new recruit to serve before transiting to a permanent post was reduced from 6 to 3.[34] The plan to corporatise certain departmental functions was shelved.[35] The change of civil service policy smoothed the political team's relations with the civil service unions.

Nevertheless, even civil servant interviewees viewed that it was not a good development under Tsang administration that more civil servants were appointed as POs. Civil-servant-turned POs were seen as being good at policy implementation and responding to short-term public concerns, but were less able to identify long-term objectives.[36] While outsider POs with little political experiences had to take some time to learn how the government works, they brought in new ideas and expertise.[37] Yet, it was getting difficult to attract competent outsiders to the government due to the adversarial political environment and lack of trustworthy politicians.[38] This is confirmed by some political appointee interviewees:

> The least appealing part [of the job] is the lack of private life. ...The property purchase that my relative made, would be now used as a political weapon against administration. That I feel really bad. [39]

The POs working in the government were also less able to initiate new policies because of the difficulty to form consensus among stakeholders. Under Tsang administration, there were only 174 bills being submitted to the LegCo during 2005/06-2011/12 compared to 338 bills being submitted to the LegCo by Tung administration during 1998/99-2004/05.[40] Despite more political appointees joining the government under the PAS and more collaborative political-administrative relations, the capacity of Tsang administration to make policy changes was not greatly improved compared to Tung administration.

Notes

1 Article 45 stipulates that, '*The method for selecting the Chief Executive shall be specified in the light of the actual situation in the Hong Kong Special Administrative Region and in accordance with the principle of gradual and orderly progress. The ultimate aim is the selection of the Chief Executive by universal suffrage upon nomination by a broadly representative nominating committee in accordance with democratic procedures*'.
2 Article 68 stipulates that, '*The method for forming the Legislative Council shall be specified in the light of the actual situation in the Hong Kong Special Administrative Region and in accordance with the principle of gradual and orderly progress. The ultimate aim is the election of all the members of the Legislative Council by universal suffrage*'.
3 Hong Kong public opinion research institute. Citizens' satisfaction towards Hong Kong SAR government. https://www.pori.hk/pop-poll/government/h001.html
4 New.gov.hk. Wong Yan-lung named Secretary for Justice. 20 October 2005. https://www.news.gov.hk/isd/ebulletin/en/category/lawandorder/051020/html/051020en08004.htm
5 Interview with a former ExCo member, 11 May 2020.
6 Interview with a former PO, 6 October 2009.
7 Interview with a former ExCo member, 11 May 2020.
8 Interview with a former Principal Official, 6 October 2009.
9 Interview with a former senior civil servant. 30 July 2009.
10 Speech by Prof Arthur K C Li, Secretary for Education and Manpower of HKSARG at the Education Forum for Asia, 2005 Annual Conference. http://www.asia-edu.org/EN/NewsCenter_View.asp?classid=75&id=369&parentclassid=

11 Hong Kong 2007-08 Policy Address. https://www.policyaddress.gov.hk/07-08/eng/policy.html
12 Interview with a former senior official. 28 August 2009.
13 Biography. Hong Kong government press release. 25 June 2021. https://www.info.gov.hk/gia/general/202106/25/P2021062500412.htm
14 Interview with a senior civil servant. 8 July 2010.
15 Speech by Secretary for Economic Development and Labour. 1 April 2004. https://www.info.gov.hk/gia/general/200404/01/0401190.htm
16 Interview with a PO, 23 October 2009.
17 Resolution passed by the LegCo on 10 December 2008. https://www.legco.gov.hk/yr08-09/english/sc/sc_lcm/general/sc_lcm.htm
18 If the project is in the public interest, don't fear public-private-collaboration. Hong Kong Economic Times. 9 September 2009.
19 Ibid.
20 Interview with a senior official, 23 October 2009.
21 LegCo Council Panel on Education. LC Paper No. CB(2)1233/09-10(01). 12 April 2010.
22 Government Press Release. Internet Learning Support Program to Launch in July. 27 June 2011.
23 iProA co-founded eInclusion in collaboration with the Boys & Girls Club. Statement by the iProA about the Internet Learning Support Program (in Chinese). LC Paper No. CB(1)2325/10-11(03).
24 Internet Learning Support Programme (ILSP): Submission to the IT and Broadcasting Panel by Mr Jeremy Godfrey, former Government Chief Information Officer (GCIO). LC Paper No. CB(1)2299/10-11(01). May 2011.
25 Internet Learning Support Programme (ILSP): Submission to the IT and Broadcasting Panel by Mr Jeremy Godfrey, former Government Chief Information Officer (GCIO). LC Paper No. CB (1)2299/10-11(01). May 2011.
26 Interview with former Under Secretaries, 28 July 2010; 6 May 2019.
27 Interview with a political assistant, 24 August 2010.
28 Interview with a political assistant, 11 August 2010.
29 Interview with a political assistant, 24 August 2010.
30 Interview with two political assistants, 28 April, 11 August 2010.
31 Interview with political assistants (3 August; 24 August; 28 August 2010); interview with a former non-official member of the government advisory body (13 December 2018).
32 Interview with a senior civil servant. 24 May 2010.
33 An Overview of the Civil Service. LegCo Panel on Public Service. LC Paper No. CB(1) 1001/10-11(03).
34 Revision to the '3+3' Civil Service Entry System. Legislative Council Panel on Public Service. LC Paper No. CB(1)2304/09-10(01).
35 Interview with a senior civil servant. 4 June 2010.
36 Interview with a senior civil servant. 6 July 2010.
37 Interview with a senior civil servant. 8 July 2010.
38 Interview with a senior civil servant. 17 June 2009.
39 Interview with a political assistant. 24 August 2010.
40 2014 Evaluation Report of Hong Kong SAR Governance. SynergyNet.

References

BBC News (2010) *Hong Kong Five Pan-democrats in the Legislative Council Formally Announced 'General Resignation'* (in Chinese). 26 January. https://www.bbc.com/zhongwen/trad/china/2010/01/100126_hongkong_democracy

Branigan, T. (2008) *Democrats Lose Seats but Retain Veto Power in Hong Kong Elections*. 8 September. https://www.theguardian.com/world/2008/sep/08/hongkong. china.

Burns, J. P. and Li, W. (2015) The Impact of External Change on Civil Service Values in Post-Colonial Hong Kong. *The China Quarterly*, 222(June), pp. 522–546.

Cheng, J. Y. S. (2011) Challenge to the Pro-democracy Movement in Hong Kong: Political Reforms, Internal Splits and the Legitimacy Deficit of the Government. *China Perspectives*, 2, pp. 44–60.

Cheng, L. (2021) A look at Hong Kong Elections and Political Reforms over Two Decades. *South China Morning Post*. 5 March. https://www.scmp.com/news/hong-kong/politics/article/3124278/look-hong-kong-elections-and-political-reforms-over-two

Cheung, G. (2005) Tsang at East Ahead of Campaign Blitz. 28 May. *South China Morning Post*.

Civic Party (2009) *Opinions on the Consultation Document about the Methods of Electing Chief Executive and Legislative Council in 2012*. Legislative Council Document CB(2) 486/09-10(02).

China News Service (2007) *Tsang Yam-kuen Announced Election Manifesto and Promised to Deliver in Five Policy Areas (in Chinese)*. 22 March. Ifeng.com

Chinese University of Hong Kong (2020) *The Identity and National Identification of Hong Kong People Survey Results*. https://ccpos.com.cuhk.edu.hk/wp-content/uploads/2020/07/The-Identity-and-National-Identification-of-Hong-Kong-People-ENG.pdf

Chung, T. Y. (2005) *The Public Opinion 'Honeymoon' Enjoyed by Tsang Ying-Kuen (in Chinese)*. https://www.hkupop.hku.hk/english/columns/columns87.html

Constitutional and Mainland Affairs Bureau (2007) *Report on Further Development of the Political Appointment System*. October https://www.cmab.gov.hk/en/issues/pa_report.htm.

Fenghuang Net (2007) *Tsang Yam-kuen Announced the Election Platform and Five Policy Outlines (in Chinese)*. 22 March. https://news.ifeng.com/special/zengyinquan/congzheng/200703/0322_868_91963.shtml

Fong, B. C. H. (2014) Executive-Legislative Disconnection in Post-colonial Hong Kong: The Dysfunction of the HKSAR's Executive-dominant System, 1997–2012. *China Perspectives*, 1, pp. 5–12.

Government Press Release (2005) *Govt's Proposed Package on 2007/08 Elections Surely Not Step Backward in Democratic Development*. 18 December.

Government Press Release (2007) *Response to US Report on Human Rights: Statement Ungrounded and Untrue*. 7 March.

Hong Kong General Chamber of Commerce (2008) *Submission on Nutrition Labelling*. 2 May. https://www.chamber.org.hk/en/advocacy/policy_comments.aspx?ID=29

Lam-Knott, S. (2018) Anti-Hierarchical Activism in Hong Kong: The Post-80s Youth. *Social Movement Studies*, 17(4), pp. 464–470.

Lee, E. W. Y. (2010) The Politics of Minimum Wage Legislation in Hong Kong: Critical Social Policy Change in a Semi-Democracy. *International Journal of Policy Studies*, 1(1), pp. 109–127.

Legislative Council (2005) *Meeting of Panel on Food Safety and Environmental Hygiene. Background Brief*. LC Paper No. CB(2) 1263/04-05(01).

Legislative Council Secretariat (2009) *Panel on Constitutional Affairs: Updated Background Brief for the Special Meeting on 26 November*. LC Paper No. CB(2)349/09-10(01).

Legislative Council Secretariat (2013) *Information Note: Housing Supply in Hong Kong. IN20/12-13.* 28 May. https://sc.legco.gov.hk/sc/www.legco.gov.hk/yr12-13/english/sec/library/1213in20-e.pdf.

Leung, A. and Cheung, G. (2005) Tsang Shows His Hand (and So Do the Big Names Backing Him). 26 May. *South China Morning Post.* https://www.scmp.com/article/502011/tsang-shows-his-hand-and-so-do-big-names-backing-him?module=perpetual_scroll_0&pgtype=article&campaign=502011.

Leung, P. (2008) Food Retailers Appeal to Public in Bid for Labelling Law Exemption. 26 April. *South China Morning Post.* https://www.scmp.com/article/635310/food-retailers-appeal-public-bid-labelling-law-exemption.

Rating and Valuation Department (2022) *Price Indices by Class (Territory-wide) (from 1979).* 27 April. https://www.rvd.gov.hk/en/publications/property_market_statistics.html.

South China Morning Post (2008) *Labelling Exemption Voted Down.* 29 May. https://www.scmp.com/article/639442/labelling-exemption-voted-down.

Sung, Y-W (2018) 'Becoming Part of One National Economy: Maintaining Two Systems in the Midst of the Rise of China.' In Lui, T-l., Chiu, S. W. K. and Yep, R.(eds.) *Routledge Handbook of Contemporary Hong Kong.* Abingdon, Oxon; New York, NY: Routledge, pp. 66–289.

Wong, H. and Chan, S-m. (2019) The Impacts of Housing Factors on Deprivation in a World City: The Case of Hong Kong. *Social Policy and Administration*, 53(60), pp. 872–888.

Yuen, S. and Chung, S. (2018) Explaining Localism in Post-handover Hong Kong: An Eventful Approach. *China Perspectives*, 3, pp. 19–29.

5 Causal paths to varied political-administrative relations in policymaking

5.1 Qualitative comparative analysis

The chapter adopts the method of qualitative comparative analysis to identify causal paths to varied political-administrative relations in policymaking during Tung and Tsang administrations (Ragin, 2014). A Boolean analysis of 18 cases presented in the previous chapters has been conducted, and the values of five causal conditions and case outcome are presented in Table 5.1.

$$R = A + ABC + BE + BD \qquad (5.1)$$

There are four conditions for R: A, ABC, BE and BD. This means that if any of these conditions is satisfied, there will be collaborative political-administrative relations. ABC refers to the condition where A, B and C are present. BE refers to the condition where B and E are present. BD refers to the condition where B and D are present.

If r indicates the adversarial political-administrative relations, then,

$$r = ABCE + ABC + B + BE + BCD$$

ABCE and ABC (or ABCe) can be reduced to ABC; BE and B (or Be) can be reduced to B. The equation can be rewritten as

$$r = ABC + B + BCD \qquad (5.2)$$

Equation (5.2) has three causal conditions: ABC, B and BCD. This means that if any of these conditions is satisfied, adversarial political-administrative relations occur. ABC refers to the condition where A, B and C are present. BCD refers to the condition where B, C and D are present.

According to the Boolean approach, from Equation (5.2), B (intensive public mood) is both a sufficient and necessary condition for the adversarial political-administrative relations.

DOI: 10.4324/9781003195924-5

Table 5.1 Truth table with five causal conditions[a]

	Similar backgrounds	Intensive public mood	Uncertainty	Multiple jurisdictions	Technical capability	Collaborative political-administrative relations
Case 2.1: Increasing housing supply	0	0	0	0	0	0
Case 2.2: Education reform	1	1	1	0	1	0
Case 2.3: Decision not to prosecute Aw Sian	1	1	1	0	1	0.5
Case 3.1: Electronic road pricing	0	1	0	0	1	0
Case 3.2: Construction and Demolition Waste Charging Scheme	0	1	0	0	1	0
Case 3.3: Reforming senior secondary school education	0	1	0	0	1	1
Case 3.4: Home ownership policy change	1	0	0	0	0	1
Case 3.5: The National Security Bill	1	1	1	0	0	1
Case 3.6: Authorising betting on football	0	1	0	0	0	0.5
Case 3.7: Sponsoring Harbour Fest	0	1	1	0	0	0
Case 3.8: Containing SARS epidemic (I)	1	1	1	1	1	1
Case 3.8: Containing SARS epidemic (II)	0	1	0	0	0	1
Case 4.1: Proposing electoral reforms	1	1	0	1	0	1
Case 4.2: Legislating mandatory nutrition labelling	0	0	0	0	1	0.5
Case 4.3: Regional Education Hub	1	1	0	0	0	1
Case 4.4: Adopting Statutory Minimum Wage	1	1	1	0	0	1
Case 4.5: Revitalising Industrial Building Scheme	1	1	1	0	0	0
Case 4.6: Internet Learning Support Programme	0	1	0	0	0	0

Source: The author.

In Table 5.1, 1=presence of the condition; 0 = absence of the condition.

For R, 1 = presence of collaborative political-administrative relations; 0.5 = presence of mutually respectful political-administrative relations; 0 = adversarial political-administrative relations.

A = political appointees/political executives and senior civil servants have similar career or professional backgrounds.

B = the issue involves intensive public mood, namely a high level of attention by members of Legislative Council or interest groups or the general public.

C = when the issue is a new problem with no proved solutions.

D = when the issue is under the purview of multiple political appointees.

E = when political appointees have technical capability of handling the issue.

If R-r indicates the mutually respectful political-administrative relations,

$$r = B + BE \tag{5.3}$$

From Equation (5.3), B is both a sufficient and necessary condition for the mutually respectful political-administrative relations.

5.2   Refining hypotheses

Based on the three equations, some of the original hypotheses developed in Chapter 1 are refined:

H3a (refined): Similar career or professional background between political appointees and civil servants is a sufficient but not necessary condition for *collaborative political-administrative relations in policymaking.*

H4a (refined): The fact that the issue involves intensive public mood is a necessary and sufficient condition for *adversarial or mutually respectful political-administrative relations in policymaking.*

H4b (refined): When the issue is new with no proved solutions and involves intensive public mood, similar career or professional backgrounds between political appointees and civil servants are associated with either *adversarial or collaborative political-administrative relations in policymaking.*

H4c-1: When the issue is under the purview of multiple political appointees and involves intensive public mood, the political-administrative relations will be *collaborative in policymaking.*

H4c-2: When the issue is under the purview of multiple political appointees, involves intensive public mood and is new with no proved solution, the political-administrative relations will be *adversarial in policymaking.*

H4d (refined): When political appointees have technical capability of handling the issue and the issue involves intensive public mood, the political-administrative relations in policymaking can be *either collaborative, adversarial or mutually respectful.*

The outcome of H3a, H4b and H4d is more than one. There could be alternative causal conditions that account for a specific outcome. The new hypotheses about alternative causal conditions will be proposed from the case analysis.

5.2.1   *Alternative causal conditions: political uncertainty and supportive/critical public mood*

Comparing cases featuring similar causal conditions but a different outcome helps to identify alternative causal conditions.

Cases 3.5, 4.4 and 4.5 are related to H4b-1.

Comparing Cases 3.5 and 4.5, conditions A, B and C are present in both cases, but the outcome is different. In Case 3.5, the National Security Bill proposed by the government had weak public support, but the Bill was mandated by the Central People's Government (CPG). Therefore, the political risks were clearly born by the political appointees and CPG. It was less likely that civil servants objected to this initiative. By contrast, Revitalising Industrial Building Scheme (Case 4.5) was a local initiative led by a bureau secretary. Civil servants perceived that they might bear the risks of being criticised to collude with real estate interests, while the rewards of successfully making and implementing the policy were uncertain. From the two cases, the level of uncertainty in political costs and benefits perceived by civil servants is identified as an alternative causal condition for varied political-administrative relations. The following hypothesis is proposed:

H4e: when the level of political uncertainty is perceived high by civil servants, the political-administrative relations in policymaking will be adversarial.

Comparing Cases 4.4 and 4.5, conditions of A, B and C are present in both cases, but the outcome is different. In Case 4.4, legislating statutory minimum wage (SMW) obtained majority support among the public and the surveyed senior civil servants, even though the legislating process involved open conflicts between employees and employers, and high degree of uncertainty in terms of SMW's impact on economy. By contrast, in Case 4.5, there was no clear majority support from the public or LegCo for the new scheme and at the same time the public mood was critical of civil servants collaborating with real estate interests. The different nature of intensive public mood is identified to account for the different outcome of two cases. Similarly, in Cases 3.7 and 3.4, supportive and critical public mood, in conjunction with the condition about actors' career background, were associated with collaborative and conflictual political-administrative relations in policymaking. Two sub-hypotheses are proposed:

H4b-1: When the issue is new with no proved solutions (technical uncertainty) and the public mood is supportive, similar career or professional backgrounds between political appointees and civil servants will be associated with their collaborative political-administrative relations in policymaking.

H4b-2: When the issue is new with no proved solutions (technical uncertainty) and the public mood is critical, despite similar career or professional backgrounds between political appointees and civil servants, political-administrative relations will be adversarial in policymaking.

5.2.2 *Alternative causal condition: policy goal sharing*

Cases 3.1, 3.2, 3.3 and 4.2 are related to H4d.

Comparing Cases 3.1, 3.2 and 3.3, conditions B and E are all present in these cases, but the outcome of Cases 3.1 and 3.2 is different from the outcome of Case 3.3. In Cases 3.1 and 3.2, the political appointee was an 'outsider' who had technical capability to handle the issues, and would like to initiate the policy despite the risk of invoking critical public mood. In both cases, the issues were perceived by civil servants to have risks of invoking critical public mood that could jeopardise their career. The outcome of two cases (adversarial political-administrative relations in policymaking) is consistent with H4e.

By contrast, in Case 3.3, although the political appointee and the senior civil servant had different career and professional backgrounds, they shared policy goals of reforming senior secondary school education despite the critical public mood. This is consistent with the Expanded Principal-Agent Model that proposes political appointees (principal) may share goals with civil servants (agent). Similar to Cases 3.1 and 3.2, the political appointee in Case 3.3 had technical capability to handle the issue. A sub-hypothesis of H4d is proposed:

H4d-1: When political appointees have technical capability to handle the issue, and political appointees and civil servants share policy goals, despite their different career and professional backgrounds and critical public mood, their working relations in policymaking will be collaborative.

In the refined H4a,[1] the outcome for 'intensive public mood' (condition B) is unclear. In three cases (Cases 2.1, 4.6 and 3.6) where condition B was present, the alternative condition 'policy goal sharing' explained a different outcome of the cases. In Cases 2.1 and 4.6, the political appointees (including CE) and civil servants had different policy goals; their working relations in policymaking were adversarial. By contrast, in Case 3.6, while the issue was not the priority of the political appointee, but civil servants' policy preferences had support from superior politicians (policy goal sharing), the political-administrative relations in policymaking were mutually respectful. In all three cases, the public mood was critical.

Therefore, the following hypotheses are proposed in relation to H4a-1 (refined):

H4a-1: When the issue involves critical public mood, and there is no policy goal sharing between political appointees and civil servants, the political-administrative relations in policymaking will be adversarial.

H4a-2: When the issue involves critical public mood, and there is policy goal sharing between some but not all superior political appointees and civil servants, the political-administrative relations in policymaking will be mutually respectful.

5.2.3   Alternative causal condition: blame shifting

In the original H4b[2] in Chapter 1, the causal condition between 'the issue is new with no proved solutions' (condition C) and 'adversarial and collaborative working relations with the civil servants' (outcome R) is proposed to be 'the political appointees will spend efforts on controlling policymaking'.

It is found that in Cases 2.2, 3.5, 3.8(I) and 4.5, political appointees indeed sought to control policymaking. However, in Cases 3.7 and 4.4, political appointees chose to shift blame to civil servants, regulatees and a statutory body, respectively, with a different outcome of political-administrative relations in policymaking.

In Case 3.7, political appointees delegated the programme to civil servants, rather than controlling the latter. Therefore, the causal condition is the intention of political appointee to shift blame by the public about the failure of the programme to the civil servant who oversaw the programme implementation (see Chapter 3).

In Case 4.4, similar career background between the political appointee and civil servants enhanced the trust between them in managing the political uncertainty related to the legislation. The evidence that wage protection movement did not produce the desirable outcome successfully shifted the blame for legislation to the regulatees: the employers. The delegation of setting the hourly minimum wage to a statutory body (Minimum Wage Commission) was a strategy to minimise public blame on political appointees and civil servants for setting a specific level of wage.

The causal condition 'political appointees shifting blame' is found in both Cases 3.7 and 4.4. The following hypothesis is proposed:

> H4b-3: When the issue is new with no proved solutions (technical uncertainty), and political appointees shift blame to civil servants for the policy failure, the political-administrative relations in policymaking will be adversarial.
>
> H4b-4: When the issue is new with no proved solutions (technical uncertainty), and political appointees shift blame to other parties for the policy failure, the political-administrative relations in policymaking will be collaborative.

5.2.4   Alternative causal condition: ministerial responsibility

In the original H4c[3] in Chapter 1, the causal condition between 'the issue is under the purview of multiple political appointees' (condition D) and 'the adversarial/collaborative/mutually respectful relations in policymaking' (outcome R) is 'the lead political appointee would find it difficult to control subordinate civil servants'.

In Cases 3.7, 3.8 (II) and 4.1, the issue was under the purview of multiple political appointees, but the case outcome was different.

In Case 3.7, the political appointee who made the decision left the government when that decision was implemented. The decision was later criticised by the public. The succeeding political appointee failed to fulfil his responsibility to oversee the implementation of that decision, nor to defend the civil servant involved in its implementation. Instead, the adversarial political-administrative relations in policymaking were resultant from the blame politics between the succeeding political appointee in charge and the civil servant being criticised by the LegCo.

In Case 3.8 (II), the Secretary for Health Welfare and Food (SHWF) delegated the coordinating emergency tasks to the civil servants, and resigned from the post to take the blame by the critical public. The ministerial responsibility taken by the SHWF explained the collaborative political-administrative relations in this case.

In Case 4.1, reforming the electoral system for the development of democracy was one of the five agendas in CE's election manifesto. The chair and a member of the Task Force in charge of the electoral reform were AO-turned political appointees, the same as CE. The importance attached by the CE to this issue and the support by two political appointees strengthened ministerial responsibility for the proposal. The resultant political-administrative relation in policymaking was collaborative.

The causal mechanisms in Cases 3.8 (II) and 4.1 have the commonality of 'political appointees shouldering ministerial responsibility'. The following hypotheses are proposed:

H4c-1: When the issue is under the purview of multiple political appointees who shoulder ministerial responsibility, the political-administrative relations in policymaking will be collaborative.

H4c-2: When the issue is under the purview of multiple political appointees who fail to shoulder ministerial responsibility, the political-administrative relations in policymaking will be adversarial.

5.2.5 *Alternative causal condition: true political leadership*

In the original H4d[4] in Chapter 1, apart from 'political appointees having technical capability of handling the issue' (condition E), another causal condition for 'the collaborative or mutually respectful political-administrative relations in policymaking' (outcome R) is 'political appointees would like to control policymaking'.

However, although in all the cases where E is present, the political appointees would like to control policymaking, only in Cases 3.3 and 4.2, the case outcome was consistent with R.[5] In Cases 2.2, 3.1 and 3.2, the case outcome was 'adversarial political-administrative relations in policymaking'. The commonality of these cases is that the 'outsider' political appointees were driven by their professional ideals and exercised 'true political leadership' despite opposition by civil servants and their interest group allies. The 'true political leadership' is modelled as an executive acting on his/her private information which suggests that a popular policy choice is not truly in the public interest, without fearing the possible political loss (such as losing an election) (Canes-Wrone, Herron and Shotts, 2001).

For instance, in Case 2.2 (Education reform), the permanent secretary viewed that the outsider political appointee '*had no historical baggage and would help to see things [education reform] from an objective perspective*', whereas the civil servants (education officers) '*grew up with many principals in the frontline*', and when the policy was unpopular to the school sector, these civil servants '*very often would say, you know it's not my decision*' and '*started to retreat from giving the full picture*'.[6] Similarly, in Cases 3.1 and 3.2, the outsider political appointee was aware of, but did not mind the political uncertainty involved in the issues, and went ahead to formulate and implement the policies, because her five-year term in the government '*gave her a sense of urgency to move things quickly*'. Only after she '*made many enemies*', she realised that '*time is important to politics. If there is not enough time, the risk can be high*'.[7]

The following hypothesis is proposed:

H4d-2: When the 'outsider' political appointees have technical capability of handling the issue and exercising true political leadership, the political-administrative relations in policymaking will be adversarial.

5.3   An adjusted analytical framework

Based on the Boolean analysis and comparative case analysis, the causal conditions presented in Table 5.1 are adjusted and added as follows:

Condition B: Intensive public mood. It is revised to include '*critical public mood*' and '*supportive public mood*'. The condition of 'supportive public mood' is reflected in hypotheses H4b-1 and H4b-2 (Section 5.2.1).

Condition C: Uncertainty. It is revised to include '*new issues with no proved solution*' (technical uncertainty) and '*issues with high probability of inviting critical public mood*' (political uncertainty). The second condition is reflected in hypothesis H4e (Section 5.2.1).

'*Policy goal sharing*' is added as an alternative causal condition. The condition is reflected in H4d-1, H4a-1 and H4a-2 (Section 5.2.2).

'*Blame shifting by political appointees*' is added as an alternative causal condition, and is reflected in H4b-3.

'*Shouldering ministerial responsibility*' is added as an alternative causal condition, and is reflected in H4c-1 and H4c-2.

'*True political leadership*' is added as an alternative causal condition, as is reflected in H4d-2.

Taking reference to Ostrom's Institutional Analysis and Development Framework, the causal conditions are organised at three levels in the adjusted analytical framework (Figure 5.1).

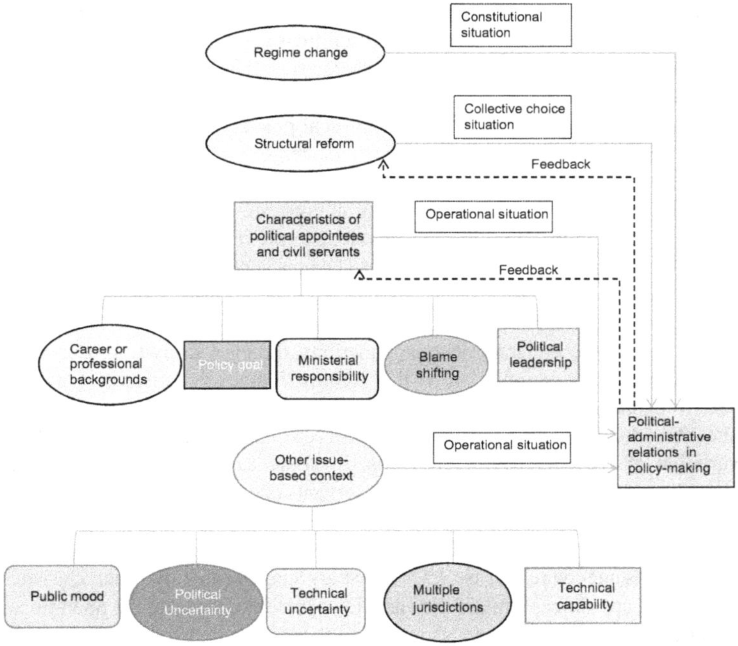

Figure 5.1 An analytical framework explaining political-administrative relations in policymaking at three levels (II).

Source: The author.

5.4 Theoretical and practical implications

Based on a qualitative comparative case analysis, this book proposed a framework that synthesised several theories and models mostly developed and applied in Western democratic contexts, to explain varied political-administrative relations in policymaking in a hybrid regime with colonial legacy, a Confucian administrative tradition and a high degree of policy and administration autonomy under China's unitary and socialist system. These theories and models include role-perception models, Public Service Bargains (PSB), accountability relation models, political-administrative relations in policymaking, social structure theory, neo-institutionalism and Institutional Analysis and Development Framework. The case analysis findings and the proposed framework have the following theoretical and practical implications:

First, while the change of PSB from the colonial trustee-type to the post-colonial agency type was initially unstable, resulting in adversarial relations between the Chief Executive (top political executive) and senior civil servants, the structural reforms (POAS and PAS) strengthened political control over policymaking by introducing political appointees from outside the government in place of civil servant secretaries. The post-reform PSB was gradually stabilised during Tsang administration when more civil servants were appointed to the newly created political positions, and the civil service autonomy in personnel and financial management was to some extent restored. The economic recovery during Tsang administration enabled the government to address civil servants' material concerns and stabilise the agency bargains. The findings are consistent with the previous studies that changes of PSBs are responses to environmental changes such as economic crisis, and such responses are diverse and shaped by the existing institutions (Lodge and Hood, 2012; Hansen, Steen and de Jong, 2013).

Second, at the collective choice situations, the case study (e.g. Cases 3.2 and 3.7) confirms the proposition that reform changes from trustee-type bargain to agency-type bargain are likely to result in cheating and blame avoidance (Hood, 2002). However, the impacts of reforms on PSB have considerable variation at the operational situations. In some cases, political appointees shouldered the blame even though civil servants cheated when exercising their discretionary power (e.g. Case 3.8 [I]). In other cases, political appointees were prepared to take blame even though civil servants cheated by not supporting the former's agenda (e.g. Case 4.5). The study suggests that two characteristics of political appointees explain the variation of reform impact at the operational situations: (1) willingness to shoulder ministerial responsibility (to take the blame); (2) willingness to exercise true political leadership (to adopt unpopular policies). These characteristics are consistent with Confucian tradition of expecting mandarins to uphold high ethical standards and be responsible for their subordinate's fate and long-term interests of the governed (Chau, 1996).

Third, the analysis of political-administrative relations in specific policymaking context helps to identify the linkage between actors' role perceptions and their behaviour, filling in a gap of previous studies that applied the role-perception model. While the four images of political-administrative relations are ideal types, they assume stable interaction between politicians and bureaucrats who understand and accept each other's role. However, the case analysis suggested that different images of political-administrative relations in specific policymaking situation would lead to their distrustful and adversarial working relations. For instance, in Case 3.2, the civil servant behaved like the Classical Bureaucrat in Image I (Putnam, 1973; Gregory, 1991), who was reactive in programme commitment and had low tolerance of political conflicts, while the 'outsider' political appointee had the expertise and was eager to and capable of controlling policymaking, like politicians in Image IV (Aberbach et al., 1981). In the end, political appointee perceived that their working relation 'did not work out'.[8]

Fourth, inconsistent with the social structural theory and neo-institutionalist theory, the case analysis showed that career civil servants were responsive to changes in the political environment after taking up the political appointment.

They initiated politically controversial reforms demanded by the CPG (Case 3.5) and local political parties (Case 4.1). They changed the beliefs of non-intervention in the market under the political pressure to correct market failure problems such as low wages (Case 4.4) and housing shortage (Case 4.5). The study found that civil-servant-turned political appointees changed the incremental policymaking styles traditionally found in Hong Kong government (Scott, 2010), and were more responsive to short-term political demands and partisan interests than before (Cases 3.4 and 4.6). The case analysis identified the impact of the POAS and PAS reforms on the beliefs and policy preferences of civil-servant-turned POs despite the persistence of civil service values carried over through political appointment and Civil Service Code. The effect of career and professional backgrounds on political-administrative relations varied at the individual level, rather than the structural level. Therefore, in Figure 5.1, the condition of actors' career and professional backgrounds is categorised as an institution at the operational situation (characteristics of political appointees and civil servants), rather than at the collective choice situation. There is also feedback of the reforms at the operational situation.

Fifth, the analysis found that conflicts between politicians and civil servants could arise from their obligations to act according to different types of accountability. Politicians' exercises of different types of political accountability also have different consequences for political-administrative relations. In Case 4.6, the strengthened political accountability requirements of the political appointees were in conflict with the professional accountability and legal accountability requirements of the civil servant. The political appointees' intervention in the civil servant's decision-making was perceived to be accountable for narrow partisan interests, and was considered by the civil servant as being illegitimate. By contrast, in Case 4.5, the political appointee intended to be politically accountable for the risky decision, which was accepted by the civil servants.

Sixth, the transaction cost theory assumes that the uncertainty costs of legislative rule-making only involve unexpected rule compliance requirements placed upon the constituents. This study identifies civil servants as a body of constituents who are affected by the unexpected costs due to public criticism of the enacted policy (political uncertainty). Therefore, the strengthened political control over policymaking in an adversarial political environment makes some civil servants more risk-averse in policymaking. The findings confirm what Romzek (2000) had suggested; in designing government reforms, reformers need to align accountability practices with the culture and behaviours the reforms seek to encourage, such as willingness to take risk and innovate.

Notes

1 H4a (refined): The fact that the issue involves intensive public mood is a necessary and sufficient condition for adversarial or mutually respectful political-administrative relations in policymaking.

2 H4b: When the issue is new with no proved solutions, the political appointees will spend efforts on controlling the policymaking, leading to his/her adversarial or collaborative working relations with the civil servants.

3 H4c: When the issue is under the purview of multiple political appointees, the lead political appointee would find it difficult to control subordinate civil servants, leading to the former's adversarial or collaborative or mutually respectful relations with the latter in policymaking.

4 H4d: When political appointees have technical capability of handling the issue and would like to control policymaking, their working relations with civil servants are likely to be collaborative or mutually respectful.

5 The different outcome of two cases is consistent with H4d-1 and H4d-2 proposed in Section 5.2.2.

6 Interview with a former senior civil servant. 30 July 2009.

7 Cheung Chi-fai and Olga Wong. Civil servants can be too inflexible, says Sarah Liao. *South China Morning Post.* 3 July 2007.

8 Interview with a former PO, 3 August 2009.

References

Aberbach, J. D., Putnam, R. D. and Rockman, B. A. (1981) *Bureaucrats and Politicians in Western Democracies.* Cambridge, Mass.: Harvard University Press.

Canes-Wrone, B., Herron, M. C. and Shotts, K. W. (2001) Leadership and Pandering: A Theory of Executive Policymaking. *American Journal of Political Science,* 45(3), pp. 532–550.

Chau, D. M. (1996) Administrative Concepts in Confucianism and Their Influence on Development in Confucian Countries. *Asian Journal of Public Administration,* 18(1), pp. 45–69.

Gregory, R. (1991) The Attitudes of Senior Public Servants in Australia and New Zealand: Administrative Reform and Technocratic Consequence? *Governance: An International Journal of Policy, Administration and Institutions,* 4(3), pp. 295–331.

Hansen, M. B., Steen, T. and de Jong, M. (2013) New Public Management, Public Service Bargains and the Challenges of Interdepartmental Coordination: A Comparative Analysis of Top Civil Servants in State Administration. *International Review of Administrative Sciences,* 79(1), pp. 29–48.

Hood, C. (2002) Control, Bargains and Cheating: The Politics of Public Service Reform. *Journal of Public Administration Research and Theory,* 12(3), pp. 309–332.

Lodge, M. and Hood, C. (2012) Into an Age of Multiple Austerities? Public Management and Public Service Bargains across OECD Countries. *Governance: An International Journal of Policy, Administration and Institutions,* 25(1), pp. 79–101.

Putnam, R. D. (1973) The Political Attitudes of Senior Civil Servants in Western Europe: A Preliminary Report. *British Journal of Political Science,* 3(3), pp. 257–290.

Ragin, C. C. (2014) *The Comparative Method: Moving Beyond Qualitative and Quantitative Strategies.* Berkeley: University of California Press.

Romzek, B. S. (2000) Dynamics of Public Sector Accountability in an Era of Reform. *International Review of Administrative Sciences,* 66, pp. 21–44.

Scott, I. (2010) *The Public Sector in Hong Kong.* Hong Kong: Hong Kong University Press.

6 Implications for political-administrative relations in policymaking 2012–2022

6.1 Implications for political-administrative relations during Leung Chun-ying administration (2012–2017)

Before being appointed as Hong Kong government's Chief Executive (CE) in July 2012, Leung Chun-ying was a professional surveyor and a non-official member of the Executive Council (1997–2002), the most important advisory body for the CE and administration (Xinhua News Agency, 2020). When Leung assumed office, he faced challenging issues such as widening wealth gaps, increasing demand for health care and elderly care by an aging population, unaffordable private housing and insufficient provision of public housing, public aspiration for selecting CE and Legislative Council members by universal suffrage immediately, and competition with other cities in the region (Luo and Cheng, 2013).

Although Leung was an 'outsider', his working relations with civil servants were said to be collaborative. This was confirmed by a senior government advisor:

> The relations between government civil servants and political appointees of this administration has improved a lot. Although they still proposed opposing opinions, but finally implemented the political appointees' decisions. They do it. In the past, when Sarah Liao Sau-tung was the Secretary, civil servants boycotted her decisions. They did not do.[1]

Compared to Tsang Yam-kuen's second administration (see Chapter 4), Leung appointed fewer number of career civil servants to be Principal Officials (POs). Among 15 POs nominated by Leung for Central People's Government to appoint, seven were former civil servants, including five career administrative officers (AOs) and two officers in the departmental professional grade (Table 6.1). All of the rest POs were professionals working in the private sector, including one in the mass media. However, only two of these POs used to be affiliated with local political parties, and only one was elected

DOI: 10.4324/9781003195924-6

Table 6.1 Principal Officials (policy secretaries) of HKSARG[a] in July 2012

Position titles in July 2012	Career background	Political party affiliation before taking the position
Chief Secretary for Administration	A career AO in HKSARG	Nil
Financial Secretary	A career AO in HKSARG	Nil
Secretary for Justice	A private legal professional	Nil
Secretary for Education	A private sector human resource management professional	Nil
Secretary for Commerce and Economic Development	A private legal professional	former deputy chair of Democratic Alliance for the Betterment and Progress of Hong Kong
Secretary for Constitutional and Mainland Affairs	A career AO in HKSARG	Nil
Secretary for Security	A career immigrant officer in HKSARG	Nil
Secretary for Food and Health	A medical professional and public health system manager	Nil
Secretary for the Civil Service	A career AO in HKSARG	Nil
Secretary for Home Affairs	A journalist and newspaper editor	Nil
Secretary for Labour and Welfare	A career AO in HKSARG	Nil
Secretary for Financial Services and the Treasury	A university professor	Nil
Secretary for Development	A career engineer in HKSARG	Nil
Secretary for the Environment	A private architect	Nil
Secretary for Transport and Housing	A university professor and senior manager, and former non-official member of Executive Council and former member of colonial Legislative Council	former founding deputy chair of Democratic Party

Source: Central Gov't appoints new HKSAR team, 28 June 2012. Hong Kong Government news website. https://www.news.gov.hk/en/categories/admin/html/2012/06/20120628_095212.shtml

as a Legislative Councilor (LegCo) in the colonial government. As a private surveyor, Leung lacked local mass electoral experiences nor did he have reliable political support in the LegCo.

Leung nominated two career AOs to be the highest-ranking POs, the Chief Secretary for Administration (CSA) and Financial Secretary (FS). This showed that he still relied on experienced AOs to move the government machine and lead political work in policy processes.

The public mood was critical during Leung's administration. Public opinion polls showed that people on average tended not to trust the Hong Kong government and CPG during 2014–2017.[2] CE's major initiatives such as reorganising the government structure, increasing the land supply for housing and implementing work projects and even budget bills were delayed or shelved due to filibuster in LegCo.[3] Filibuster referred to 'deliberately creating situations of meetings being adjourned due to a lack of quorum and proposing motions to adjourn proceedings', and thereby 'deliberately impeding the Government's implementation of policies' (Government Press Release, 2016). The situation worsened after the umbrella movement in late 2014.[4] Compared to the 2012–2013 LegCo session when it took an average of 1.12 hours for the LegCo Finance Committee to vet and approve an item, as of 13 May 2016, the average time required for vetting and approving an item in LegCo multiplied to 3.21 hours (Government Press Release, 2016). The FS found it difficult to get the budget bill passed by the LegCo timely, warning that the recipients of social security would suffer because of the delay (Chan, 2014). According to H4b-4[5] (Chapter 5), the political-administrative relations could be collaborative because both political appointees and civil servants blamed LegCo's filibuster for inefficient government performance during Leung's administration.

While the author did not have the first-hand data about how senior civil servants perceived their roles during Leung's administration, since the CS and FS were career AOs, their policy styles of balancing sectoral interests and belief in sustainable public finance would not be in conflict with senior civil servants in policy bureaus. On the agenda of formulating a universal retirement protection plan, the CE acknowledged that unsustainable public finance, difficulty to introduce new taxes in the era of global competition and a lack of consensus between employers and employees were hurdles.[6] In 2014, when a government-commissioned research report suggested adopting a universal demo-grant partly financed by the government fund and partly financed by a progressive old age tax in 2014,[7] the Working Group on Long-Term Fiscal Planning (the Working Group) chaired by the Permanent Secretary for Financial Service and the Treasury (Treasury) issued two reports forecasting a structural deficit in between 7 to 15 years, given different expenditure scenarios. The FS stressed that there was little room for tax hikes in order to maintain the competitiveness of Hong Kong, and the government needed to contain expenditure and lived within its means.[8] To support the CE's proposal

of establishing and accumulating an 'elderly care fund' in his election campaign platform,[9] the FS set aside 50 billion HKD for retirement protection of
the elderly in need. At the same time, the FS took recommendations from the
Working Group and established a future fund in 2016.[10]

Despite CE being an outsider and the criticism of some Legislative Council
members,[11] his working relations with civil servants in formulating a universal
retirement protection plan were collaborative, thanks to their similar beliefs
about Hong Kong's fiscal situation and the difficulty to form consensus between different interests.

6.2   Implications for political-administrative relations during Lam Cheng Yuet-ngor administration (2017–2022)

Although Lam was a career AO, among 16 POs (with policy portfolios) nominated by her, only six were career AOs. Two POs were career civil servants
from professional grades. Three POs were promoted from the positions of
Under Secretary (see Table 6.2). All but one of these POs were working as
civil servants or political appointees in the government at the time of appointment (China Search Net, 2017). This showed that Lam preferred to appoint
existing officials with experiences and track records.

Different from a typical career AO who upholds the principle of fiscal
discipline, in her election platform, Lam pledged that the government should
play a proactive role of facilitating and promoting, 'invest' in the future of
Hong Kong, and share the fruit of economic development with the general
public (Da Kung Net, 2017).

Lam's administration, however, was challenged to serve an increasingly
polarised and politicised society. Some localists who supported Hong Kong's
independence from China and militant protests (Yuen and Chung, 2018) won
seats in 2015 District Council election and 2016 Legislative Council election.
According to a public opinion survey, right before the beginning of Lam's
administration (May–June 2017), the mean score with respect to respondents'
trust in Hong Kong government was the highest (4.86[12]) since September
2014. The mean score dropped to 3.61 in May–June 2019 when 1 million
people were reported to participate in street protests against the proposed extradition bill (Jennings, 2019; Chinese University of Hong Kong, 2020). Lam
and two members of the Executive Council apologised in June 2019 about
their handling of the extradition bill (Neuman, 2019). The government announced to suspend the bill in June and withdrew the bill in August. Nevertheless, the street protests went on, and involved violence and clashes between
the protesters and the police officers. In July 2019 alone, the police force issued six press releases condemning radical protesters' illegal and violent acts
such as blocking the roads, demolishing the railings, hurling bricks, smoke
grenades and petrol bombs that set fires, attacking and injuring some police

Table 6.2 Principal Officials (policy secretaries) of HKSARG in July 2017

Position titles in July 2012	Career background	Political party affiliation before taking the position
Chief Secretary for Administration	A career AO in HKSARG	Nil
Financial Secretary	A private accountant	Nil
Secretary for Justice	A private legal professional	Nil
Secretary for Education	A career AO in HKSARG and former Under Secretary for Education	Nil
Secretary for Commerce and Economic Development	A career AO in HKSARG	Nil
Secretary for Constitutional and Mainland Affairs	A career AO in HKSARG	Nil
Secretary for Security	A career police officer and former Under Secretary for Security	Nil
Secretary for Food and Health	A university professor	Nil
Secretary for the Civil Service	A career AO in HKSARG	Nil
Secretary for Home Affairs	A former Legislative Councilor	former deputy chair of Democratic Alliance for the Betterment and Progress of Hong Kong
Secretary for Labour and Welfare	A university professor	Nil
Secretary for Financial Services and the Treasury	Former Under Secretary for Financial Services and the Treasury, a former senior manager in statutory bodies, a former AO in HKSARG	Nil
Secretary for Development	A career AO in HKSARG	Nil
Secretary for the Environment	A private architect	Nil
Secretary for Transport and Housing	An electronics engineer officer in HKSARG and former Director of Electrical and Mechanical Services	Nil
Secretary for Innovation and Technology	A private sector electronics engineer and general manager, a former university administrator	Nil

Source: Baidu Encyclopedia, China Search Net (2017).

officers while the latter dispersed the unlawful assembly.[13] According to a media report, by mid-September 2019, more than 1,300 people had been arrested during the clashes between protesters and police.[14]

Lam's original priorities stated in the election campaign platform did not include legislating Article 23 of Basic Law to safeguard national security in Hong Kong, but concerned local and regional social-economic development issues (Xinhua, 2017). In a media interview after Lam left the government, she admitted that she did not anticipate that the proposed extradition bill[15] would have led to violent protests and social-political instability during 2019–2020 (South Net, 2022).

The political-social instability during 2019–2020 was associated with increasing crime rates in some categories. For instance, in 2019 compared to 2018, the number of arson cases increased 219.7% and the number of burglary cases increased 52%.[16] Many civil servants participated in the street protests and some were involved in the illegal acts related to the protests. For instance, during June to November in 2019, the government received complaints about 43 civil servants participating in illegal assemblies (Haiwai Net, 2019). On 2 August 2019, civil servants were reported to attend a rally expressing demands that the government should withdraw the extradition bill, investigate police misconduct and resume political reforms (Hunt, 2019). A civil servant in the Immigration Department was arrested and charged to have stolen personal information of about 200 police officers and sent them to the doxxing websites (Lever, 2021).

The conflicts between politics and administration during Lam's administration were in the form of civil servants protesting against government extradition bill and police officers' use of force. There were also contestations over the meaning of political neutrality. The Civil Service Code stipulates that civil servants are required to uphold the value of political neutrality, which means '*civil servants shall serve the CE and the Government of the day with total loyalty and to the best of their ability, no matter what their own political beliefs are*'.[17] However, at a public rally held on 2 August 2022, the former Secretary for Civil Service Mr Wong Wing-ping stated that 'political neutrality' did not mean civil servants should be personally loyal to the CE, but meant that civil servants should be loyal to the system and indirectly to the public (Wang, 2019).

Wong's interpretation of political neutrality was not accepted by the Hong Kong government, who soon issued a public statement, clarifying that

> when civil servants express their views, they should ensure that their views would not give rise to any conflict of interest with their official duties, or might not be seen to compromise the important principle of maintaining impartiality and political neutrality when discharging their duties.
>
> (Government Press Release, 2019a)

Some civil servants' contestation of the extradition bill and police's actions was so intense that new rules about the loyalty of civil servants and public officers were formulated and enforced. In 2020 Policy Address, Lam stressed that all civil servants joining the government on or after 1 July 2020 must sign a declaration to uphold the Basic Law, swear allegiance to the HKSAR[18] of the People's Republic of China and be responsible to the HKSAR government. In May 2021, a law requiring all public officers, including LegCos and District Councilors, to take the oath, was passed (Xinhua, 2021). By June 2022, a total of 129 Hong Kong civil servants and 535 other government workers have been sacked or resigned after failing to take the oath (Hunt, 2022).

On 24 November 2019, there was a record high turnout rate (71.23%) of voters in the District Council election[19] and the opposition camp won nearly 90% of the District Council seats.[20] In January 2020, the Chinese Communist Party (CCP) Center replaced Wang Zhimin as the Director of the Liaison Office of CPG with Luo Huining, who was a CCP provincial committee party secretary. Luo's appointment indicated that the Party Center assumed direct leadership over Hong Kong's administration (Burns, 2022). In April 2020, when the protests and riots were still going on, the CE Lam recommended the CPG to change five POs in response to the political crisis (Xinhua News Agency, 2020).

Lam changed Secretary for Civil Service. The new Secretary for Civil Service was Patrick Nip Tak-kuen, the former Secretary for Constitutional and Mainland Affairs. Nip implemented the civil service oath-taking measures. During the time when some civil servants openly challenged government decisions, implementing these measures involved high level of political uncertainty. At the same time, there was political support from pro-establishment LegCos[21] and the CPG,[22] which reduced political uncertainty for policymakers. In light of H4e[23] (Chapter 5), the political-administrative relations in implementing the controversial oath-taking measures could be adversarial.

Lam replaced the Secretary for Home Affairs (SHA), with an Under Secretary for Labour and Welfare (Caspar Tsui Ying-wai) who had the same political party background. District Council election is one of the portfolios of SHA. The Chinese government media People's Net criticised that too many opposition camp's members were qualified to be 2019 district council election candidates (People's Net, 2019). At the same time, civil servants (the Returning Officers) received public criticism and doxxing when making decisions to disqualify one nominated candidate on the grounds that he advocated self-determination and independence in order to challenge the constitutional status of Hong Kong as an inalienable part of the People's Republic of China (Government Press Release, 2019b).

After the adoption of the Hong Kong National Security Law (the Law) on 30 June 2020, the Registration and Electoral Office disqualified more nominees from the opposition camp attending the 2020 LegCo election (Global Times, 2020). By 1 February, 2021, 97 persons were arrested for suspected commitment of crimes under the Law, such as secession, subversion, terrorist activities, collusion with a foreign country or with external elements and so on (Government Press Release, 2021). By 21 October, 55 elected District Councilors had been disqualified and 260 had resigned in anticipation of disqualification due to their invalid oath-taking (CGTN, 2021; UK Foreign, Commonwealth & Development Office, 2022). After Lam shouldered ministerial responsibility to replace the POs, and sought political support from the CPG to restore law and order in Hong Kong, civil servants (e.g. Returning Officers) were able to collaborate with political appointees to enforce the Law that had been politically controversial. Similar to the logic in H4c-1[24] (Chapter 5), the political-administrative relations in enforcing the Law and related legislation were collaborative.

6.3 Conclusion and discussions

The study concludes that when the handover of power to govern Hong Kong replaced a trustee-type public service bargain with an agency-type bargain, a structural reform (the POAS) was introduced to emphasise more political accountability than bureaucratic accountability, and to shift the policymaking role from civil service to political executives.

The POAS reform expanded the role differentiation between political appointees and civil servants, and consequently the political-administrative relations in policymaking were diverse depending on the political and administrative actors' characteristics (not just backgrounds) and other issue-based context. The study found multiple conditions that account for the collaborative, mutually respectful and adversarial political-administrative relations in policymaking.

The conditions concerning political-administrative actors' characteristics include the following:

First, similar career or professional backgrounds between political appointees and civil servants.

Second, whether or not political appointees share policy goals with civil servants.

Third, whether or not political appointees are willing to shoulder ministerial responsibility.

Fourth, whether or not political appointees shift blame to civil servants or other parties.

Fifth, whether or not political appointees exercise true political leadership, modelled as executives not choosing a popular policy that is not truly in the public interest (or choosing an unpopular policy that is truly in the public interest).

The conditions concerning other issue-based context include the following:

First, whether the issue involves critical or supportive public mood.

Second, whether the level of political uncertainty is perceived high by civil servants.

Third, whether the issue is new with no proved solutions (technical uncertainty).

Fourth, whether the issue is under the purview of multiple political appointees (multiple jurisdictions).

Fifth, whether political appointees have technical capability to handle the issue.

The study concludes that the POAS and PAS reforms have enabled political executives to implement policy goals that differ from senior civil servants' long held beliefs in the 'small government, free market' doctrine. Values and policy styles of senior civil servants such as political neutrality, fiscal prudence and avoiding political risks (e.g. delaying legislating local national security laws) were somewhat preserved through civil service regulations and political appointment (Burns and Li, 2015; Li, 2022), which constrained the political team from proactively meeting the changing demands of the local community and the expectations of CPG.

The POAS and PAS reforms have also cultivated senior civil servants with political ambition, and changed their values and policy styles through political appointment. One AO-turned PO explained how the political position enabled her to take risks and make a difference:

Hands on my heart, I wouldn't probably be advocating the same in both [policy] packages have I not been a PO, a political appointed official who could stand up and be held responsible for taking that particular action. ... I felt very strongly that I was personally responsible for these packages. I was quite prepared to say sorry publicly if I got wrong this time. With that, perhaps my senior and my counterparts felt that since there was a body with this strong commitment to be held responsible, they would allow me to do it. ...But in the civil service mindset and operating environment, perhaps that will be difficult.[25]

As Scott pointed out (2005, p. 185), policy processes in post-colonial Hong Kong have been influenced by stakeholders with diverse interests and values outside the government. As a result, senior officials within the government have been less able to control the choice of policy solutions. The case analysis in Chapters 2–4 has documented what and how alternative and often conflicted values and interests in the community challenged the policy processes under the evolving political-administrative dynamics. In some cases, the outsider CE and POs opened up the policy processes to community input (e.g. Cases

2.1, 3.2 and 3.8[I]), even though their initiatives were resisted by senior civil servants. Under such circumstances, adversarial political-administrative relations constrained political appointees from responding to public demands. In other cases where public distrust in CPG was invoked, collaborative political-administrative relations often failed to produce policy proposals acceptable to the local stakeholders (e.g. Cases 3.3, 3.5 and 4.1). The findings affirm Cheung's assessment (2013) that POAS and PAS reforms had limited capacity to smooth legislative-executive relations and enhance local people's trust in Hong Kong government, which, in turn, restricted the reforms from resolving social-economic structural problems through policy changes.

Time matters. The POAS reform has been introduced for over two decades, and the political-administrative relations have been gradually evolving. The appointment of civil servants to fill the CE and PO positions and local people's general distrust towards the Hong Kong government have provided feedback that changed the past governing philosophies and policy styles of senior civil servants. Ironically, the political crisis related to the extradition bill in 2019–2020 enabled the local political team to mobilise political support from the CCP Center to create, reinterpret and enforce civil service regulations, upholding hierarchical loyalty as one of the most important civil service values. Hong Kong's evolving political-administrative dynamics after the structural reforms is consistent with the theory of gradual institutional change: institutional stability and changes are outcome of actors' ongoing political contestation over the meaning, application and enforcement of ambiguous rules that have implications for resource distribution (Mahoney and Thelen, 2010).

The study has a number of limitations.

First, the assignment of values to causal conditions in Table 6.1 is based on the qualitative analysis of the case materials, which could be imprecise. For instance, in most cases, there is no public opinion survey data to evaluate whether the public mood is supportive or critical of the government, and whether the public paid high-level attention to the issue. In future, more in-depth and quantitative within-case analysis may help measure the value of public mood more accurately.

Second, the sample size of political appointees and senior civil servants is relatively small, particularly of those who have worked together, which limits the opportunities to triangulate the interview information. Some political executives who were unpopular with the public tended to reject the interview invitations, which biased the findings of the study. The busy schedules of interviewees also restrict their interview time and amount of information to be shared with the investigators. The study lacks sufficient interview information about the political-administrative working relations during Leung Chun-ying and Lam Cheng Yuet-ngor administrations, which leave the research questions open to further investigations in future.

Notes

1 Interview with a senior government advisor, 8 February 2017.
2 The mean of the answers to the question 'Do you trust Hong Kong SAR (Special Administration Region) government?' was below 5 in seven surveys conducted during 2014–2017. The mean of the answers to the question 'Do you trust the Central government' was below 5 in seven surveys conducted during the same period. Zero represents 'no trust at all', 5 represents 'so so', 10 represents 'Total Trust'. Hong Kong Public Opinion & Political Development Opinion Survey, The Chinese University of Hong Kong, May 2020.
3 China News Net. Leung Chun-ying responded to the charge of selling the land of Hong Kong: Nonsense (in Chinese). http://finance.cnr.cn/gundong/201210/t20121001_511039426.shtml
4 The umbrella movement was led mainly by secondary and university student activists who opposed the decision by the standing committee of the National People's Congress made on 31 August 2014 that only allowed universal suffrage of CE from the candidates nominated by the nominating committee. The movement participants occupied some populated areas in Hong Kong Island and Kowloon and blocked traffic for 79 days (Government Press Release, 2014; Ortmann, 2015; Hayasi, 2022).
5 H4b-4: When the issue is new with no proved solutions (technical uncertainty), and political appointees shift blame to other parties for the policy failure, the political-administrative relations in policymaking will be collaborative.
6 Policy Address 2013. https://www.policyaddress.gov.hk/2013/
7 University of Hong Kong, Research Report on Future Development of Retirement Protection in Hong Kong. 20 August 2014.
8 Government press release. FS stresses need for long-term fiscal planning. 26 February 2014.
9 Full text of the new Chief Executive Leung Chun-ying's Election Platform. 25 March 2012. http://www.sina.com.cn
10 2015–2016 Budget Speech. https://www.budget.gov.hk/2015/eng/budget41.html
11 For instance, Legislative Councilor Leung Kwok-hung moved a motion debate on 5 July 2017, requesting the government to implement a non-means-tested universal retirement protection system with uniform payment. LegCo Press Release, https://www.legco.gov.hk/yr16-17/english/press/pr20170703-1.html
12 For the answers to the question 'Do you trust Hong Kong SAR government?', zero represents 'no trust at all', 5 represents 'so so', 10 represents 'total trust'.
13 Hong Kong Police Force, Police Messages, July 2019. https://www.police.gov.hk/ppp_en/03_police_message/pr/index.php?month=201907
14 Violence flares after Hong Kong protesters defy police ban. The Associated Press. https://www.uticaod.com/. 15 September 2019.
15 The formal name of the bill is 'Fugitive Offenders and Mutual Legal Assistance in Criminal Matters Legislation (Amendment) Bill 2019'. The Amendment was triggered by a suspect murder case taking place in Taiwan involving a Hong Kong citizen. The proposed Amendment intended to enable Hong Kong government to sign extradition deals with other governments who could, in turn, prosecute Hong Kong people suspected of crimes on their soil after extradition (Jennings, 2019). Many Hong Kong people and groups worried that the Amendment would allow for arrests and extradition of Chinese government critiques and dissidents to mainland China (e.g. Catholic News Agency, 2019).
16 Hong Kong Police Force, Comparison of 2019 and 2018 Crime Situation, https://www.police.gov.hk/ppp_en/09_statistics/csc_2018_2019.html
17 Hong Kong Civil Service Bureau. https://www.csb.gov.hk/english/admin/conduct/1751.html

18 Special Administration Region.
19 2019 District Council Election Voter Turnout Rate, https://www.elections.gov.hk/dc2019/eng/turnout.html.
20 France 24, Hong Kong election delivers landslide win for pro-democracy camp. 25 November 2019. https://www.france24.com/en/20191125-hong-kong-carrie-lam-election-democracy-china
21 The Legislative Councilor Regina Ip moved a motion to the Panel on Public Service of the Legislative Council, which was passed, urging the CE to issue an executive order under Article 48(4) of the Basic Law to require all civil servants to swear to uphold the Basic Law and swear allegiance to the HKSAR of the People's Republic of China.
22 In November 2020, the Standing Committee of National People's Congress (NPCSC) stated that a LegCo member does not fulfil the legal requirements and conditions on upholding the Basic Law and pledging allegiance to the HKSAR of the People's Republic of China if the member advocates or supports 'Hong Kong independence', refuses to recognise the People's Republic of China's sovereignty over Hong Kong and the exercise of the sovereignty, solicits intervention by foreign or external forces in the HKSAR's affairs, or carries out other acts that endanger national security. *Decision about the qualifications of Hong Kong SAR Legislative Council members by NPCSC.* 11 November 2020. Xinhua News Agency.
23 H4e: When the level of political uncertainty is perceived high by civil servants, the political-administrative relations in policymaking will be adversarial.
24 H4c-1: When the issue is under the purview of multiple political appointees who shoulder ministerial responsibility, the political-administrative relations in policymaking will be collaborative.
25 Interview with a former PO, 23 October 2009.

References

Burns, J. P. (2022) The Chinese Communist Party in Hong Kong. King Faisal Center for Research and Islamic Studies, *Special Report*, June.

Burns, J. P. and Li, W. (2015) The Impact of External Change on Civil Service Values in Post-Colonial Hong Kong. *The China Quarterly*, 222(June), pp. 522–546.

Catholic News Agency (2019) *Hong Kong Extradition Bill Could Further Endanger Christians, Advocates Say.* 17 June. https://www.catholicnewsagency.com/news/41570/hong-kong-extradition-bill-could-further-endanger-christians-advocates-say.

Chan, K. (2014) *Tsang Rules Filibuster to End before Friday.* 22 May. https://www.chinadailyasia.com/hknews/2014-05/22/content_15136405.html.

Cheung, A. B. L. (2013) Public Governance Reform in Hong Kong: Rebuilding Trust and Governability. *International Journal of Public Sector Management*, 26(5), pp. 421–436.

CGTN (2021) *12 Hong Kong District Councilors Disqualified.* 21 May. https://news.cgtn.com/.

China Search Net (2017) *21 Senior Officials of Carrie Lam Cheng Yuet-ngok Administration Have Been Selected and Waiting for Appointment* (in Chinese). https://news.sina.com.cn/c/gat/2017-06-01/doc-ifyfuvpm6985868.shtml.

Chinese University of Hong Kong (2020) *Hong Kong Public Opinion & Political Development Opinion Survey*, May. https://ccpos.com.cuhk.edu.hk/wp-content/uploads/2020/07/Hong-Kong-Public-Opinion-and-Political-Developments-ENG.pdf.

Da Kung Net (2017) *Lam Cheng Yuet-ngok Announced the Election Platform and Proposed Three Major Areas of Administration.* 4 February. http://www.hkstv.tv/index/detail/id/48717.html.

Global Times (2020) *Wong Chi-fung was Disqualified to Compete in the LegCo Election; Hong Kong Legal Professional: Deterring Hong Kong's Independence* (in Chinese). July 30. https://news.sina.com.cn/c/2020-07-31/doc-iivhuipn5979875.shtml.

Government Press Release (2014) *LCQ2: Selecting CE by Universal Suffrage.* 12 November. https://www.info.gov.hk/gia/general/201411/12/P201411120937.htm.

Government Press Release (2016) *Impacts of Filibusters on Government's Implementation of Policies and HK Society.* 18 May 2016. https://www.fstb.gov.hk/en/news/legco/docs/pr20160518_e.pdf.

Government Press Release (2019a) *Interpretation of Principle of Political Neutrality of Civil Service.* 3 August. https://www.info.gov.hk/gia/general/201908/03/P2019080300860.htm.

Government Press Release (2019b) *HKSAR Government Responds to Media Enquiries Regarding 2019 District Council Ordinary Election.* 29 October. https://www.info.gov.hk/gia/general/201910/29/P2019102900256.htm.

Government Press Release (2021) *Law and Order Situation in 2020.* 2 February 2021. https://www.info.gov.hk/gia/general/202102/02/P2021020200749.htm.

Haiwai Net (2019) *43 Civil Servants Were Investigated-Hong Kong Government: It Would Not Be Allowed (in Chinese).* 27 November. https://news.sina.com.cn/c/2019-11-27/doc-iihnzahi3710322.shtml

https://new.qq.com/rain/a/20191028A0A7RG00

Hayasi, N. (2022) *When It Rains It Pours: The Umbrella Movement in Hong Kong.* 4 May. http://the nonviolence project.wisc.edu.

Hunt, M. (2019) *Hong Kong Civil Servants Join Protests against Extradition Bill.* https://www.globalgovernmentforum.com/hong-kong-civil-servants-join-protests-against-extradition-bill/.

Hunt, M. (2022) *Hong Kong Civil Servants Defy Allegiance Oath.* 23 June. https://www.globalgovernmentforum.com

Jennings, R. (2019) *How an Obscure Taiwan Murder Case Led to Hong Kong's Mega-Protests.* 19 June. https://www.latimes.com/world/la-fg-taiwan-china-hong-kong-chan-tong-kai-murder-20190619-story.html

Lever, R. (2021) What Is Doxxing? https://www.usnews.com/360-reviews/privacy/what-is-doxxing.

Li, W. (2022) Does Politicized Public Service Appointment Strengthen Political Control over Policy Advice? The Case of Hong Kong, China. *Policy Studies.* https://www.tandfonline.com/doi/full/10.1080/01442872.2022.2133103

Luo, J-y. and Cheng, J. Y-s. (2013) *An Analysis of Tsang Yam-Kuen's Era-A Chess Game left to Leung Chun-ying.* Hong Kong: Hong Kong City University Press.

Mahoney, J. and Thelen, K. (2010) 'A Theory of Gradual Institutional Change.' In Mahoney, J. and Thelen, K. (eds.) *Explaining Institutional Change: Ambiguity, Agency, and Power.* Cambridge: Cambridge University Press, pp. 1–37.

Neuman, S. (2019) *Hong Kong Leaders Apologize for Extradition Bill as They Brace for More Protests.* https://www.npr.org/.

Ortmann, S. (2015) The Umbrella Movement and Hong Kong's Protracted Democratization Process. *Asian Affairs,* XLVI(I), pp. 32–50.

People's Net (2019) *Warning! These People Can Be Qualified (for election)! What Shall Be Done with Hong Kong's District Council Election* (in Chinese). 2 November. http://hm.people.com.cn/n1/2019/1102/c42272-31434164.html

Scott, I. (2005) *Public Administration in Hong Kong: Regime Change and Its Impact on the Public Sector.* Singapore: Marshall Cavendish Academic.

South Net (2022) *Lam Cheng Yuet-ngor's First Media Interview after Completing the Term Speaking about Her Experiences as a HKSARG Chief Executive (in Chinese).* November 10. https://news.southcn.com/node_4538da31bd/2d71697f43.shtml.

UK Foreign, Commonwealth & Development Office (2022) Hong Kong Councillors: Foreign Secretary's statement. https://www.gov.uk/government/news/foreign-secretary-statement-on-hong-kong-councillors.

Wang, R. (2019) It Is Necessary to Reiterate the Principle of Political Neutrality for Hong Kong Civil Servants (in Chinese). August 6. https://www.sohu.com/a/331742595_115479

Xinhua (2017) *Lam Cheng Yuet-ngor Vows to Uphold 'One Country, Two Systems' Principle, Work for HK Progress.* http://english.cctv.com/2017/04/11/ARTIWbbKC-5MjmLqof5lY5Zwq170411.shtml.April 11.

Xinhua (2021) HK Law Requiring Civil Servants to Take Oath Comes into Effect. *China Daily.* May 21.

Xinhua News Agency (2020) *The State Council Removes and Appoints Principal Officials of Hong Kong SAR Government* (in Chinese). April 22. http://www.gov.cn/xinwen/2021-06/25/content_5620782.htm.

Yuen, S. and Chung, S-h. (2018) Explaining Localism in Post-handover Hong Kong: An Eventful Approach. *China Perspectives*, 3, pp. 19–29.

Appendix I

Summary of survey and interview samples

Type of respondents	Number and periods of responses

Political appointees	5 interview responses (year 2016–2019)
	  – Directors of bureaus (2)
	  – Under Secretary (1)
	  – Political assistants (2)
	19 interview responses (year 2009–2012)
	  – Directors of bureaus/policy secretaries (13)
	  – Under Secretary (1)
	  – Political assistants (5)

Civil servants	78 survey responses:
	  – departments 29 (year 2016.10–2017.1), bureaus 49 (year 2019.3-5)
	37 interview responses:
	  – 27 (year 2009–2012), 10 (year 2017.1–2019.4)

External expert and policy advisors	41 interview responses (year 2016.3–2019.12)
	  – Non-official members of ASBs (8)
	  – Consultants, researchers in universities, think tanks and NGOs (28)
	  – Researchers of Hong Kong Legislative Council (4)
	  – Assistant to a Legislative Council member (1)
	79 survey responses (non-official members of ASBs) (year 2018.3-12)

Total	Interview responses: 102; Survey responses: 157

Source: Politician-bureaucrats Project (2009–2012); Policy Advisory System Project (2016–2019).

Reproduced from the article accepted by the 'Policy Studies' journal.

Appendix II

Summary of survey and interview instruments

Politician-bureaucrats Project (2009–2012)	
Political appointees semi-structured interviews (2009–2012)	10 open-ended questions, 7 close-ended questions (including 26 five-point-Likert-Scale sub-questions)
Civil servants semi-structured interviews (2009–2012)	10 open-ended questions, 7 close-ended questions (including 26 five-point-Likert-Scale sub-questions)

Policy Advisory System Project (2016–2019)	
Civil Service Survey (2016–2019)	15 questions (including 14 five-point-Likert-Scale sub-questions). Invitation for interviews (5–7 open-ended questions) at the end of the survey
Non-official members of ASBs[a] Survey (2018)	18 questions (including 13 five-point-Likert-Scale sub-questions). Invitation for interviews (5–7 open-ended questions) at the end of the survey
Political appointees semi-structured interviews	13 survey questions (including 11 closed ended questions and 14 five-point-Likert-Scale sub-questions) 5–7 open ended questions for discussions
Researchers of Legislative Council semi-structured interviews	9 survey questions (including 8 close-ended questions, 5 five-point-Likert-Scale sub-questions)
External expert and policy advisors interviews	4 open-ended questions

Source: Politician-bureaucrats Project (2009–2012); Policy Advisory System Project (2016–2019).

Reproduced from the article accepted by the 'Policy Studies' journal.

[a] Advisory and Statutory Bodies.

Index

For Product Safety Concerns and Information please contact our EU
representative GPSR@taylorandfrancis.com
Taylor & Francis Verlag GmbH, Kaufingerstraße 24, 80331 München, Germany